P9-BTM-358

11/23
STRAND PRICE
$ 5.00

BIRDERS

By the same author

A Himalayan Ornithologist (with Carol Inskipp)
Richard Meinertzhagen
Loneliness and Time
Rivers of Blood, Rivers of Gold

BIRDERS

Tales of a Tribe

MARK COCKER

Atlantic Monthly Press
New York

Copyright © 2001 by Mark Cocker

All rights reserved. No part of this book may be reproduced in
any form or by any electronic or mechanical means, including
information storage and retrieval systems, without permission
in writing from the publisher, except by a reviewer, who may
quote brief passages in a review. Any members of educational
institutions wishing to photocopy part or all of the work for
classroom use, or publishers who would like to obtain
permission to include the work in an anthology, should
send their inquiries to Grove/Atlantic, Inc.,
841 Broadway, New York, NY 10003.

First published in Great Britain in 2001 by Jonathan Cape
Random House, London

Published simultaneously in Canada
Printed in the United States of America

The extract in chapter five by Bill Oddie (*Birdwatch,* October
1998) is reproduced with the kind permission of the author.

FIRST AMERICAN EDITION

Library of Congress Cataloging-in-Publication Data

Cocker, Mark, 1959–
    Birders : tales of a tribe / Mark Cocker.
      p. cm.
    ISBN 0-87113-844-1
    1. Bird watching. 2. Bird watchers. I. Title.

QL677.5 .C588 2002
598'.07'234—dc21   2001056490

Atlantic Monthly Press
841 Broadway
New York, NY 10003

02 03 04 05   10 9 8 7 6 5 4 3 2 1

For all those who stayed at 104 Unthank Road,
especially Richard and Helen,
and for our absent friends, Alan Adams and Maggie Gorn

Contents

Acknowledgements

The preparation and writing of this book have given me greater pleasure than any previous work. And why wouldn't they? All birders love to talk and reflect on their life's passion and my research essentially involved lengthy conversations with about forty fellow devotees.

During these discussions I recorded their (and my own) memories and thoughts on almost every aspect of birding culture. Many of the people I spoke with are distinguished participants in that world, many of them are friends. But all of them were unfailingly considerate in sharing their ideas and in helping to shape the book. Without that kindness and assistance the task literally would have been impossible and I owe them an enormous debt of gratitude.

The group includes Bryan Bland, Clive Byers, Richard Campey, Robin Chittenden, Nigel Collar, Graeme Cresswell, Alan Eardley, John Fanshawe, Dick Filby, Paul Flint, Steve Gantlett, Mark Golley, Derek Goodwin, Chris Heard, Christopher Helm, Dave Holman, Ron and Sue Johns, John Kemp, Guy Kirwan, Paul Lewis, Duncan McDonald, Tony Marr, Pete Milford, Richard Millington, Derek Moore, Richard Porter, Nigel Redman, Craig Robson, Steve Rowland, Terry Stevenson, Caroline Still, Tony Stones, Ian Wallace, Cliff Waller, Stuart Winter and Barbara and Martin Woodcock.

However I wish to offer special thanks to Clive Byers and Ron and Sue Johns, whose advice and opinions I sought on many more occasions. I am particularly indebted to them for enduring a constant barrage of enquiries on a whole range of seemingly trivial issues.

Many people made important contributions in a whole range of other ways. First amongst these is Steve Whitehouse, who helped to set the ball rolling and who gave sound advice and clear recollections on a number of matters. I also wish to mention Gary Allport, Chris Batty, Arnoud van den Berg, Paul Dukes, Mike Edgecombe, Jonathan Elphick, Dave Farrow, Steve Gantlett,

Helen and Richard Grimmett, Dave Holman, Chris Kightley, Tom Lowe, Rod Martins, Chris Mead, Howard Medhurst, Andrew Raine, Barry Reed, Mike Rogers, Tim Sharrock, Steve Snelling, Moss Taylor, Lars Svensson, Ian Wallace and Richard Webb. Adam Gretton was another of those whose thoughtful advice I sought routinely and whose kind help was freely given. My old friend Tony Hare discussed many aspects of the book and offered his critical judgement on some of the writing. To all of them I give my sincerest thanks.

Although they may not be mentioned explicitly in the text, there are a number of old friends who were present with me in the field at the time of the experiences I describe. To these named and unnamed companions, some of whom I haven't seen for a quarter of a century, I would like to pay belated tribute. In rough chronological order they are: John Mycock (Tog), Mark Beevers, Jim Lidgate, Kevin Hughes, Alan Jones, Paul Flint, Alan Wood, Barbara Holmes, Aileen Alderton, Miriam Barnett, Brenda Ferris, Denise Huckle, Colin Beckett, Ros Gibbon, Jonathan Benn and Debbie Chubb and, of course, the late Alan Adams.

There are a small number of permanent 'fixtures' in my book writing. These are my agent Gill Coleridge and my editor Dan Franklin, who first said, 'You must write it.' They helped hugely in setting up and shaping the initial project, then gave me crucial encouragement during the writing. As always, I am deeply indebted to them both. I would also like to thank the excellent staff at Cape for all their hard work, especially Jason Arthur, Kate Harbinson and Suzanne Dean.

Finally I must acknowledge the invaluable support, both at work and off duty, that I received from my wife, Mary, and our two girls, Rachael and Miriam. They helped in too many ways for them all to be listed. However, I cannot end without mentioning the fact that pinned on my office wall is an important document entitled 'Rules for Daddy'. This includes the following: '3. Don't go out birdwatching for too long. 4. Don't stand around bird-watching while we are on a walk.' For allowing me to break these almost at will I offer them my heartfelt thanks.

Satyr Tragopan

1 male Satyr Tragopan, Tragopan satyra
Chandan Bari, Nepal, 20 May 1996

The indefinable fragrance of the Himalayas was in the air – a high sweet blend of wild flowers, dew on conifer forest and woodsmoke rising from numerous cooking hearths. We were on the southern edge of the Langtang mountains in northern Nepal and it was 20 May 1996. There were six of us up at dawn: our two guides, Ramesh and Chabindra, plus four others, including a friend, Alan, and myself.

I'd persuaded a group of seven friends, half of them members of an old birdwatching class that I'd taught for ten years, to come on a trip to look for Himalayan birds and walk through the mountains. About as tiring as a hard day's shopping in Norwich was how I'd tried to convince them they could do it. Unfortunately I'd based that assessment on my own trekking experience thirteen years earlier, when I was twenty-three. Most of my group were in their fifties and sixties. I realised too late that I needed to review my description of trekking. It still felt like shopping in the city. But more like a whole week of it . . . continuously.

The day before had been a real grind – about a 3000-foot climb (and about equivalent to ascending Ben Nevis) to a spot called Chandan Bari. Today was going to be worse. After a few hours' birding we were off up the equivalent of Nevis again, but most of it at an altitude three times the height of Britain's tallest mountain. Above 10,000 feet most Europeans find the air desperately thin. Your lungs pump frantically to filter out the necessary amounts of oxygen. Muscles grow weary and tempers fray. By the dawn of the 20th, day eleven of our trip, we were not the happiest of groups.

That morning I was most worried about Alan. Whenever he looked at me I sensed the menace in his eyes — a mixture of plotted revenge and irritation at allowing himself to be so easily fooled. Alan was fifty-eight years old, six foot four and about seventeen stone. The only small blessing was that he was getting lighter by the hour. At one point on the trail, after a steep climb, he'd arrived with sweat running in rivulets down his torso and a soaked white hanky knotted on his bald head, like Gumby out of the Monty Python sketch. He arrived with the words, 'Stuff me slowly with a yard broom.' It was his way of telling us he was shagged out and I was surprised to find he was up that dawn for the birding excursion.

But then I'd billed it as the highlight of the trek. In fact I'd even confessed that the whole thing — the tour for eight people for seventeen days, with a support staff of over twenty Nepalese — had been arranged specifically to get *me* to this spot, on this morning to look for one bird: Satyr Tragopan. I was only half joking.

Satyr Tragopan is amongst the most beautiful names for any of the world's 10,000 species of bird and a loose translation might be 'horned god of the forest'. But this is a creature even more lovely than its title. It's a type of pheasant. Those who haven't seen one shouldn't try to conjure the beast by thinking of those beautiful but stupid birds that blunder into our car windscreens. Comparing a tragopan to the hand-reared pheasants we know in Britain is like trying to evoke an Apache warrior by describing a balding overweight London businessman.

Imagine, perhaps, a bird the size of a really large cockerel with an electric blue face, erectile black feather horns that it can raise at will and a body plumage of the deepest blood red.

Overlay that magical colour with hundreds of white ocelli so bright they look luminous. Then surround each of the glowing eyes with an intense black margin and you have a sense of this extraordinary creature. And that's only the appearance.

The beauty and power of its habitat undoubtedly feed into its legend as the most sought-after bird in Nepal, a country that boasts one of the highest species totals proportional to its surface area (about 850 different birds) in the world. Tragopans occur only in dense Himalayan forest usually above 8000 feet on the steepest slopes. At Chandan Bari it was as atmospheric a spot as you could imagine – huge, widely spaced stands of hemlock, dripping with hanks of moss and lichen, the morning mist rising upwards and shredded to light ribbons by the trees' dramatic silhouettes.

As we walked through the forest away from the campsite we could actually hear a tragopan calling. That alone was amazing. The first sound was a harsh, repeated *ka-ka-ka-ka-ka-ka-ka-ka*, which had a distinctive mocking quality. Much more weird and powerful was an unearthly, un-birdlike, drawn out, rising wail, *W-a-a-a-a-a-a-a*. It was the sort of sound you would expect from a horned god of the forest. It was tantalising and magnificent, but it was not enough. And after a long and complicated stalk we all finally got to see the bird itself. For about two or three seconds it was in view as it rushed down a tree stump, from which it had been calling, and ran off over a steep brow – a blur of crimson studded with a hundred silvery eyes. We never saw it again. The horned god was gone. Yet it is still, undoubtedly, the most beautiful, wondrous and thrilling wild bird I've seen in my life.

In a sense, the purpose of this book is to explain why that tragopan is so special and to make that moment intelligible to someone who has perhaps never even been birding. It is to let you understand and feel what I felt on that May morning. I'd like you to see, for instance, why it wasn't enough simply to hear the creature. Why it was so important to continue until we were in a position for the light to make its near-instantaneous journey from the tragopan to me and on to the retina of my eyes.

The following 215 pages are no more than a description of that three-way relationship between bird, light and human observer. Because that momentary biochemical process has eventually come to be surrounded by an entire subculture and a type of tribe, with its own rules, structures, history, customs, language, etiquette and values. To help you grasp completely that moment between me and the tragopan I must explain all the elements in that society and introduce at least some of the characters who make up the tribe; the bird tribe. It's a book about the way birders' lives are defined by the experience, what they'll do and what they sacrifice to ensure it. It is, in short, about the way the human heart can be shaped by the image of a bird.

So come on . . . let's go birding. Remember – it's no more difficult than a hard day's shopping. *W-a-a-a-a-a-a-a.*

The Archaeopteryx

c.5 Feral Pigeons, Columba livia
Chapel-en-le-Frith, 1968(?)

My first concrete memories of an intense interest in birds date from about the age of eight. My father had a shop, originally for general groceries, then women's clothes and finally a launderette, in the north Derbyshire town of Chapel-en-le-Frith. Set amongst the bleak, powerful upland country of the Peak District National Park, Chapel is a quiet rural place, a commuters' retreat from the urban sprawl of Manchester a few miles down the busy A623. But it suffered then from heavy traffic coming to and from Derbyshire's numerous limestone quarries – lorries laden with huge trailers of stone and powdered lime that hurtled down Chapel's main street. Their empty wagons rattled as they pounded the road's frost-cratered surface, and as they passed our shop it shook briefly with the violent impact.

It was bitterly cold. A grey slab of cloud pressed down on Chapel's damp winter streets like a colossal lid. I can't recall why exactly we'd called at the shop or what we were doing, perhaps some kind of repairs. And I was there to help or, like small children with parents at work, allowed to think I was helping. Eventually I drifted away from the task in hand and climbed the stairs to investigate the old storeroom-attic. When I entered the room I noticed a number of slates were missing and the stark daylight was crashing in through the unhealthy cavity, scattering amongst boxes of old stock and the debris abandoned on the floor. It was just the sort of promising, wild, half-shadowed landscape that a child explorer loves. And I burrowed in.

Suddenly, from amongst this rubble of half-lit junk there came a clatter of wings, a dramatic upward surge towards the hole and, briefly, the intense silhouette of an escaping bird. Then another and another. Their departure left a swirl of dust in the shafts of cold light. They were pigeons. The usual inhabitants of parks and town centres everywhere, they had taken advantage of the building's undetected point of access and made the attic a convenient roost spot.

But I also discovered that our attic held a different kind of secret for the birds. I could smell a warm, fusty pigeon-dropping sort of odour and there was a scattering of down wafting across the floor with each blast of air. Finally, in a cavity between some broken floorboards, I unearthed several nests – shallow untidy hollows amongst heaps of crumbled plaster, old twigs, pale feathers and dry white droppings left by the birds themselves. At the centre of these crude scoops were clutches of eggs – as unexpected and exciting a discovery as any archaeologist could hope for. They lay there, pure white in colour, oval in shape, perfect amongst the winter gloom of a neglected attic.

It never occurred to me that the birds might be sitting or the eggs fertile and I rescued them from oblivion, taking them to keep in an old shoebox in a new, more comfortable nest of my own construction. For a few weeks the box and its contents were a childhood treasure, to be opened and examined after school, until they lost their compulsive numinous power and I abandoned them to devote myself to a new hobby – excavating bones from a hollow tree stump and collecting owl pellets.

I have other bird memories from after this event, but they are only a hazy background or random single-image snap-shots without context and incapable of awakening any sort of narrative. They remain suspended, jostling with a rabble of other half-remembered events, until I turned twelve, and birds stepped back into the foreground of my life. Before they asserted dominance, however, they had one last competitor to see off. I remember that for a few months I couldn't decide whether I was keener on stamp collecting or birdwatching. Very soon it was a straight race between birds and collecting stamps with birds on them. Finally it was just the birds.

From that moment until this, their place in my life is a story with a continuous plot. Yet I still go back to that winter's day in Chapel and those pigeons in an attic as a terminal point, beyond which there is absolutely nothing but darkness. That inward flood of light, that upward surge of wings, those extraordinary white eggs – they are the very earliest origins, the primeval beginnings, the *Archaeopteryx* in my personal story as a birder.

3

The Two-legged Kind

c.8 Meadow Pipits, Anthus pratensis
Lightwood Area, Buxton, March 1972

It was a standard joke when people heard I was interested in birds – 'Oh, the two-legged kind, I hope!' They said it in a mock-serious tone but with an implicit knowing wink. Then they laughed as if it were original or funny. It was neither, even to a young boy, and it was particularly irritating that it wasn't accurate. How many girls did they know with three legs?

But that kind of constant crass innuendo made me wary about disclosing my bird interests. I was especially terrified that the other two-legged kind would find out and I often rehearsed a nightmare scenario in which a large gang of girls stood in a scornful huddle laughing at the nerd with the anorak and the binoculars. I don't know why I should have had that particular childhood fantasy. At that age I didn't even know any girls.

But one of its consequences was that when I did go birding I used to slip quietly up the road to the surrounding Derbyshire moors with my binoculars concealed beneath my coat and jumper. And I always dreaded two other possibilities: one was spotting a bird I wanted to look at *before* reaching the end of the houses, where I could drop my guard. The second was meeting our next-door neighbour, Mrs Wilmott, out walking her dog, Whisky. Because Mrs Wilmott always announced to the entire street in a loud, high, singing, north-Welsh accent 'OOOH,

GOOING BIRDWATCHING ARE YOU, MAARK?' Her voice always had that note of absolute surprise, as if it was the weirdest thing in the world for a young boy to go looking at birds.

But in effect it was good old Mrs Wilmott, and my youthful embarrassment at meeting her, that really let me know at an early stage how serious I was about birding. It happened because I spotted some strange mud-brown birds feeding on an area of water-flushed pasture at a point just before the houses ended. It was inside what I considered the danger zone and staying to study the enigmatic creatures ran the distinct risk of being caught, as it were, *in flagrante delicto* by Mrs Wilmott.

But the riddle of those creatures creeping about in the tall grass was *too* strong and I had to stay to solve it. In fact I stayed several evenings, returning to the same spot to raise my binoculars, lean across the stone wall and focus in on their location. They were just a little way down the field, but my glasses converted the place into a curiously enlarged, deeply unfamiliar orbit of green.

Every now and then one of the birds would loom briefly into that intensified world. I could make out the confusing mix of streaks and bars, pale lines encircling each eye, subtle greens and browns blending with the surroundings, altering shade as the birds adopted new postures or according to the light.

I would then look up from this world and its unknown occupants and try to unearth some meaning by flicking through the pages of *The Observer's Book of Birds*. Unfortunately half the ancient plates by Archibald Thorburn were reproduced in black and white and didn't give many clues as to what lay before me. I couldn't even truly work out whether I was looking at one type of bird or several because each of them was minutely different from the next. But I'd made a startling discovery even at this primitive stage. Every bird is an individual – unique, mysterious and beautiful. It didn't really matter that I couldn't actually say what they were. I was hooked and the riddle of those strange mud-brown inhabitants of that hitherto inaccessible landscape only intensified the appeal of birding.

If someone had explained to me, as I shall now to you,

the role, the significance, the critical importance of numbers in birding, perhaps I could have been spared those nights of uncertainty, not to mention my torture at Mrs Wilmott hands. It's not just a question of the number of legs. Numbers are central to the whole business of birding. Look in a birder's notebook and all you'll find is lists of birds with numbers against each name. Numbers help you understand where you should birdwatch, which places are good for birds, what birds are rare, which common. Sometimes they even help you work out mystery species you've been attempting to unravel for days.

If I'd been told, for instance, that Meadow Pipits were one of the most numerous birds in north Derbyshire, and that there were four million breeding in Britain, but only, say, one sixtieth that number of Rock Pipits; if someone had pointed out that, numerically speaking, Meadow Pipit was 500 times more probable than Twite – like Rock Pipit, Twite was one of my candidate mud-brown species from *The Observer's Book of Birds* – I could have weighed up the possibilities and got out of there. As it was, I simply had to stick it out until the penny dropped.

So, numbers . . . let me give you some clues. About 560 bird species have been recorded in total in Britain in its entire ornithological history. But there are only about 200–225 different birds regularly breeding in this country. The rest are scarce migrants or vagrants – oddities that may only have occurred once in the last 200 years. And there's the importance of numbers already. If you have an unidentified bird in front of you, put your thoughts of the other 335 occasional, exotic species to one side. It's much more likely that you're looking at one of the commoner breeding types such as, well, Meadow Pipit.

A figure of between 200 and 250 regular species has a far wider significance in the birding world, amounting almost to a form of golden mean. It may even go some way to explain why birding has taken root in places like Britain, but not in other countries. It's certainly the number of different birds you are most likely to see in a 2–3 week trip in Britain. In fact the same rule can be extended to include two other regions of the planet that usually only birders (and a few other naturalists) bother to visit or even know about, called the Palearctic and the Nearctic.

During the nineteenth century biologists like Alfred Russel Wallace divided the planet into different faunal zones – geographical territories that share a common assemblage of animal species. Six zones are widely recognised. The Palearctic and Nearctic are two of them. All of Europe and most of Asia are included in the first of these. (Largely for administrative convenience European ornithologists have subdivided this huge landmass into the Eastern and Western Palearctic, the latter embracing Europe west of the Urals, most of the Middle East west of Iran and Africa north of the Sahara.) The complete Palearctic region stretches from the Canary Islands or Iceland in the west, across to the Pacific coast of Russia and Japan in the east. It also includes most of China north of the Himalayas.

The Nearctic is much more straightforward and incorporates all of North America to a curving line which passes just to the south of Mexico City. Sometimes, owing to the affinities that exist between bird families in the two regions, the Nearctic and Palearctic are considered together as a single super-region known as the Holarctic.

But here comes the significance of the golden average. Take any point in the Holarctic and the list of birds to be found within a radius of about 180 miles from that spot will be about 200–250. This means that in Britain, Europe and the United States – the areas of the world where birding is most popular – you'd be hard-pressed to see many more than 250 birds on a 2–3 week trip. Yet that golden mean offers you enough different birds to make it a mental challenge, sufficient variety to maintain a sense of novelty, but not so many that you're overwhelmed and confused by the sheer welter of possibilities.

It's important to realise that in terms of pure bird diversity Britain, Europe and North America are only relatively modest landscapes. There are lots of places with many more species than the golden mean. Since Archaeopteryx first appeared on earth about 145 million years ago, birds have spread and radiated outwards as a life form until there are now about 10,000 recognised species in total.

There are two basic rules in locating all this bird diversity. Species numbers decline as you rise in altitude and latitude. So, for example, in the mountains of Antarctica there are usually none at all, while lowland equatorial rainforests hold the greatest variety for any landscape on earth, with those of South America coming top. Altogether that continent holds 3100 bird species, roughly a third of the world's total on just 12 percent of its land mass. Peru and Ecuador each have national lists numbering about 1700 species. That's a greater number of different birds than in the entire Palearctic region.

Even within Britain the rules of latitude and altitude quickly come to influence birding. In Norfolk, nowhere much over 300 feet above sea-level, I've seen 134 species in twenty-four hours and the record is 159, the highest for any British county. Yet I can recall a beautiful summer's day in the Cairngorms in the Scottish Highlands, at well over 3000 feet, where we saw just *four* different birds.

There's another kind of number that impacts upon birding and it has to do with the sheer volume of birdlife. At the last count there were 148,684,606 birds breeding in Britain, give or take a few omissions and errors. And after the breeding season, including migrants, the young and non-breeding adults, there will be at least 500 million present in the country. That's more than eight birds for every single one of us. But it's when you start to calculate bird populations across whole continents that the numbers start to sound impressive.

Difficult for anyone to assess accurately, perhaps, but one person who had a go was Reg Moreau. One of the most distinguished British ornithologists in the twentieth century, Reg spent most of his working life as an agronomist in Africa. But as he lay dying of a degenerative illness in Hereford General Hospital he put the final touches to a work he hoped would be 'no bum swansong'. Don't let its technical and unwieldy title put you off. *The Palaearctic-African Bird Migration System* was a book written by a man whose imagination worked on the grand scale.

Reg was looking at those species, like the Barn Swallow and Eurasian Cuckoo, which travel out of Africa each spring heading for large parts of Eurasia, or the Palearctic, and which then reverse the journey each autumn. He tried to conceive of that chaotic sprawling mass of individual bird movements as one complete and unified process. What Moreau gave us was a breathtaking vision of overwhelming numbers reduced to the simplicity of a heartbeat, that momentous two-way passage as a mere systole and diastole in the life of Europe's migrant avifauna.

His figures are inevitably rough approximations and now a little out-of-date, but Reg speculated that the total draining through the Mediterranean and comparable latitudes further east, at the end of summer, was in the region of 5000 million birds. He also offered some figures for individual species. Try and envisage, if you can, 90 million House Martins, or 220 million Barn Swallows. When you think of Common Swifts – those black scimitar-winged lunatics that horde and scream above the city skyline – think of 200 million. And when you're exhausted by all that high-pitched screeching try to imagine the silvery falling cadence from 900 million Willow Warblers.

Hitchcock was right, but it's not a sinister nightmare. It's heaven. Birds are everywhere and, while you may not notice it, I do. So do all birders. Like them, I identify or, at least, attempt to identify every single one I see, *without* exception. I look at birds as I walk for the morning milk, when I go to the postbox, as I drive the car. I've recorded birds in the middle of the night, waking up to hear migrants flying above the house. On the day my second daughter was born I noted a flock of wild swans passing over at three in the morning. Friends have seen good birds while waiting to be served at the cheese counter in a supermarket. People birdwatch from their office. I have a pair of binoculars on my desk here, now, as I write, just in case.

Their universal presence is one reason why birds have galvanised our interest like no other life form on earth. Most birders love other aspects of wildlife, but specialising in any one of these different areas of biology is much more difficult. Botanising, for instance, is great, but tell me what you do for entertainment on a damp foggy morning in December? Butterflies are also wonderful, but try planning a field excursion on that crisp clear Saturday in February. Most birders also like mammals and many places in Africa offer a tantalising combination of fantastic birds and large game. But in Britain . . . ? The biggest predator you're likely to see is a weasel, if you're *really* lucky. Even with a night-sight and set of tunnel traps you might see, say, ten species on a good outing.

No. It's birding that offers the right balance. The range of species is good but not too great. Two hundred different birds is challenging, but not as overwhelming as, for example, the 2000 species of plant in Britain or the 20,000 insects. Then there are the other benefits. Birding is without seasonal limits. In fact, some of my favourite birding outings are winter excursions. It is this perfect combination that most birders offer as justification for their interest.

But I have a slight problem with that. To me that explains why we're not equally consumed by fungi or beetles. But it doesn't actually tackle the whole issue of *why* birds. I think it's much more to do with freedom, with notions of flight and escape, with some of our deepest fantasies, even with eroticism. But let's not talk about it. Let's go and do it . . . with the two-legged kind.

4

The Feathered Kind

1 Short-eared Owl, Asio flammeus
Goldsitch Moss, June 1972

In its infancy my birding was a completely private and unstructured interest. I had no sense of it as a collective activity, except for the odd friend who might occasionally come on a walk up the road to the moors. Nor did it occur to me that I might contribute to any formal study of local birds by sending records to a regional bird club. And I certainly never dreamed of setting myself serious study challenges, such as analysing the breeding behaviour of the Lapwing or the Woodcock.

Birding was simply a case of carefree foraging through the fields and woods around our house. Its pleasures were threefold. There was the essential joy of escape, which is so fundamental to my own birding and so enduring it's one reason I question the frequent claim people make that they watch birds because alternative branches of natural history are more limited. Birding was for me a bid for freedom. Prior to setting off each evening I can recall that the change of dress from school uniform to my old clothes felt like shedding a more restricted identity for the unlimited spaces of the Derbyshire countryside.

The second great source of happiness was a chance to go hunting. As a child my favourite forms of play were always war games, creeping around bushes with a plastic gun or stick and trying to outwit an enemy by sneaking up behind him. I'm convinced that birding at the age of twelve was a way of continuing the pleasures of an eight-year-old without appearing too ridiculous. The principle applies even thirty years later. Birding involves exactly those physical military skills of seeing and not being seen. For me this explains why so many male birders dress in paramilitary fashion – it's a subconscious expression of the boyhood soldier present in us all.

The third great pleasure was the amateur sleuthing and mental challenge involved in putting names to birds I saw. In this activity I had two basic props, a pair of cheap binoculars borrowed from my brother and my copy of *The Observer's Book of Birds*. I usually set out along one of two routes of attack. Either I wandered up the road – keeping a nervous watch for the short, jaunty frame of Mrs Wilmott – into a small wood that enveloped a reservoir on two sides. Or I would drop down to the brook which ran below our house and followed the riverbank to its origins above the wood, on an expanse of heather moorland that stretched towards Chapel-en-le-Frith on one side and the Goyt Valley on the other.

At an elevation of over 1000 feet, much of north Derbyshire is powerful country but an impoverished bird landscape. A poor local outing may produce 6 species. Even a good one may involve no more than 30–40 species. In my earliest days even this was beyond me and I usually identified around 20 birds, probably close to half those I had ever seen in my life. With such limited opportunities it's conceivable that my birding might have slowly meandered to a terminal sump on the moors around Buxton had it not received a powerful injection of enthusiasm and new experiences through joining a local natural history group in the spring of 1972.

The Buxton Field Club had been formed just after the war and, by the time I discovered it, it had already celebrated its twenty-fifth anniversary. For a young enthusiast like me it was a wonderful pool of natural historical expertise. And for its leading lights, who were often already prominent figures in a small place like Buxton, it was a further opportunity to deploy their talent and standing. The much-loved secretary, a silver-headed man with a neatly trimmed moustache, was also a local bank manager. When I met him he had held the secretarial rank for over twenty years and presided over our indoor meetings with an air of kindly military charm.

Our president, another tall, spare soldierly figure, was a senior master at one of Buxton's boys' schools. His own rank in the field club was even more enduring than the secretary's, having continued uninterrupted since 1951, while his commanding presence gave an extra air of authority to his pronouncements on natural history, especially birds, which were his main interest. But his ornithology suffered from one major setback. The man was almost completely blind; although his ears, I was told, were as sharp as a bat's.

The two senior males could not have presented a deeper contrast with the only female officer in the club. Our editor, a tiny rotund lady, was a kindly soul revered for her knowledge of plants. Unfortunately, being a birder, I was totally unreceptive to her botanical expertise and I have to confess that to an impressionable child her physical appearance and unfamiliar odour of mothballs carried an almost moral ambiguity.

On any outing her head was swathed in voluminous floral headscarves and her round frame enveloped completely in several anoraks. The parts of the body not padded with garments were consumed by a huge pair of black wellington boots. She seemed impregnable. I remember being told that her characterful country home close to the town of Chapel-en-le-Frith was entirely without amenities, such as water or electricity. I could believe it. She looked frozen. Her face was round and rubicund. Her nose was hooked and beak-like. Her piercing eyes were hooded. I suspect that had she lived in the Middle Ages she'd have had a regular ride on the ducking stool as one of the cunning folk.

Yet for sheer character our editor was outdone by the Buxton Field Club's most senior member, Dr J. Wilfred Jackson. He was an eminent local geologist and by the time I met him he was too old to accompany our field outings. In fact he was so old I remember a younger female relative had to assist even when he attended our indoor winter meetings in the back room of a Buxton pub. Occasionally the old boy would be encouraged to speak, often introducing a historical perspective on affairs. I wish I could now recall some of his memories, which stretched back well into the nineteenth century. But I have to confess my attention was less on what was said than its style of delivery, because as Dr Jackson gave his address his false teeth would lose their footings and rattle gently and continue to do so after the words had been spoken, almost like a lingering echo of the sounds enunciated. It was an unforgettable performance.

It was the field club outings, however, supervised by a younger, more dynamic corps of members, that led to a dramatic expansion in the scope of my birding. One unforgettable field trip was to Leighton Moss, a reserve belonging to the Royal Society for the Protection of Birds in north Lancashire, where there was enormous excitement when we spotted a Bittern, a bird confined to about half a dozen breeding locations. At Cannock Chase in Staffordshire we saw one of several Capercaillie, huge grouse-like birds, strutting across one of the woodland rides. They were not native to the area. The birds had been released by the Forestry Commission in the 1960s in the hope that they would re-establish themselves in the extensive conifer plantations at Cannock. But it was a forlorn project doomed to failure. Capercaillies had not been found in Staffordshire since the seventeenth century, but these niceties were lost on a twelve-year-old. I added Capercaillie to my growing list.

This and the Bittern were the rarest birds I'd seen, but they were not the most exciting or memorable from the period. That event had occurred earlier, during a more parochial outing, to the Derbyshire moors in the spring of 1972. We had gone to a spot called Goldsitch Moss, close to the A53 through north Staffordshire, a road notorious each winter for the radio and TV bulletins announcing its closure because of snowdrifts. On this particular day Goldsitch had been coaxed out of a usual clenched, wind-swept grimace by a little spring sunshine. The idea for the day was to trudge for several hours through the heather and amongst the outcrops of dark gritstone and en route listen to the Meadow Pipits performing their weak monotone cadence. Occasionally loud bubbling songs of Curlew erupted from the expanses of drab moorland.

Then someone suddenly spotted an odd bird and it was instantly apparent I'd never seen one before. It was about the size of a Curlew, yet not the same anonymous grey-brown colour and with an indefinable quality of beauty and strangeness. It floated away across the moor and then suddenly wheeled around and turned towards us, its silent and loosely bowed wings knitting a course through the updraughts in long exaggerated beats, not unlike a gigantic bat. Eventually it came much nearer, close enough, in fact, that I could see clearly two huge yellow eyes staring from within a heart-shaped facial disc.

It was a Short-eared Owl, a bird in aerial display asserting its breeding territory with that fantastic see-saw wing action. Short-eared Owls are sporadic breeders in the uplands of Derbyshire, spreading quickly in years of high vole numbers, then apparently melting away when their principal prey fails them. This bird was the first one I'd ever seen – I recall, in fact, it was my ninety-ninth species – and it was wonderful.

Before that moment I had, like every young keen birder, compensated for experiences of the real thing with long hours poring over bird books and bird pictures. But on Goldsitch Moss I realised, perhaps for the first time, by how much life can exceed imagination. A Short-eared Owl had entered my life and for those moments, as it swallowed me up with its piercing eyes, I had entered the life of an owl. It was a perfect consummation.

Birding has seldom got much better. It involved all of my three central pleasures from birds. Against the dark heather the owl assumed an almost light-radiating paleness and with its long scissoring flight action it seemed to shear from the moorland sky and make visible the abstract notion of freedom. There was also the pure joy of converting that lifeless monochrome plate from *The Observer's Book of Birds* into its living counterpart.

But here's the point of that remarkable encounter. Although the mesmerised twelve-year-old boy would never have realised it, the element which, before all others, gave the owl its shape, its luminous colour, its weightless moth-like grace, was the bird's feathers. It was the feathers which had given me, in turn, a sense of some intricately patterned and unique form, allowing me to recognise its singularity and give the beast a name. Feathers are at the core not just of a bird's appeal, but of its entire identity. In fact, strip them away from something like an owl and all you're left with is an almost foetal anonymity – the scrawny carcass of an old broiler fowl.

Feathers are the one element that all birds have shared since their Jurassic origins. In the mid-nineteenth century palaeontologists unearthed fossil imprints of reptiles with the power of flight, known as pterosaurs. But when that miraculous slab of fine-grained limestone was first opened in Solnhofen, Germany in 1861, the feature that announced the world's earliest known bird was a feather. Even 145 million years ago *Archaeopteryx* quills had acquired much of the shape, texture and structure present in all its modern descendants.

It is these that have given birds mastery of the skies and access to more of the earth's sea and land surface than any other large life form. The extraordinary insulatory properties of feathers have enabled them to travel to the very rim of survivable conditions on the planet. Alpine Chough have been discovered feeding at heights of over 24,000 feet, dancing in the wake of Himalayan mountaineers in the hope of chance scraps, while the climbers themselves are cocooned in breathing gear and thermal suits. Seabirds can comb the remotest sections of the world's oceans never bothering to land, sometimes even on the water surface, for years at a time.

I can recall once seeing an extraordinary bird – an Erect-crested

Penguin – which had arrived in the Falkland Islands in the summer of 1997. With its Chaplinesque waddle and a punk's flaring orange crest, the species normally occurs no nearer the Falklands than the sub-Antarctic islands off New Zealand. On a map I attempted to trace its course around the South Pole and the shortest route was a solo odyssey of 4000 miles. The bird could have moved along the ice shelf then hopped, island to island, fringing the Antarctic peninsula. But at some stage it *had* to cross the Drake Passage, that 600-mile stretch of ocean where the waves crest to 120 feet. I tried to imagine it navigating those seas in the monstrous darkness of the polar winter. Entirely alone.

Another species, the Emperor Penguin, reaches even greater limits of endurance. It has been known to dive for eighteen minutes achieving underwater depths of 1570 feet. Think of it: a third the height of Ben Nevis, then back to the surface in a single gulp of air.

But more incredible is the Emperor Penguin's breeding cycle, which takes place in the Antarctic winter, a feat equalled by no other bird. In fact, no other species of higher animal breeds in such forbidding conditions. At that time of year temperatures plunge to minus 40°C, while hurricane winds can drive the chill factor to minus 70°C. The male alone incubates (which involves a fast of 110–115 days, when it loses nearly half its body weight) and a single chick may be reared every two years. All this because of feathers.

These powers of survival only begin to address their miraculous properties. Flight is the one central characteristic that's made them the most studied and captivating phylum on earth. And it starts with feathers. Take an everyday British species like the Common Swift. The creature can attain a wing length of forty-eight centimetres. Yet its body weight is just forty-four grams, equivalent to a couple of Weetabix. Individually these are unremarkable statistics, but in combination they're extraordinary. In order for a man weighing 65 kilos (about ten stone) to have the same ratio of weight to wing length he'd need wings that were 635 metres long. That's almost ten times the length of a jumbo jet.

Those vital statistics mean that swifts can feed, drink, sleep and even copulate in midair. But one thing it doesn't equip them for is landing on the floor. Once grounded a swift can seldom recover the air. For that reason it never lands, except at its high rooftop nest. When a young swift leaves that birth place it can never have flown before and, once airborne, it may not land again until it starts to breed itself. That may only be after three years and some swifts are thought to remain in the ether for the entire thirty-six months.

Swifts are amazing creatures, but hummingbirds from the Americas are even more so. Their flight encompasses such levels of physical intensity it seems almost incomprehensible. Small in absolute terms, hummingbirds have breastbones and muscles that are relatively larger than on any other bird. In ordinary flight their wings beat at 22–78 times per second and in some courtship flights they may reach levels of 200 beats a second. Such is the structure of the wing that it moves freely at the shoulder in any direction, enabling the bird itself to go forward, up, down, even backwards. The inventor of the helicopter, Igor Sikorsky, said that he got many of his best ideas from watching hummingbirds. The ancient Toltecs and the Mexica worshipped them as gods.

At these intense levels of activity the heart soars to 1200 beats a minute and such is their energy consumption that hummingbirds have to feed frequently on energy-rich sources like nectar. For an adult man to achieve the same metabolic rate he would have to consume 155,000 calories a day. Despite living so precariously – and hummers literally run the risk of starvation every day – some of them, like the Rufous Hummingbird, make migration journeys of over 2000 miles and they regularly undertake single flights across the Gulf of Mexico of 600 miles. Not bad for a beast that weighs the same as a single one-pence piece.

The feathers enabling the hummingbirds' aerial feats have their origins, like all feathers, in a layer of active cells beneath the bird's skin surface. As these cells divide and subdivide they push outwards, moving progressively further from the source of nourishment and oxygen in the underlying dermis. Eventually they die off and become filled with a horny substance called keratin. As one scientist put it, feathers are 'simply an astonishingly elaborate and specialised product of the bird's epidermis . . . made of practically nothing but keratin'.

Six types have been identified, but we need concern ourselves with just one – contour feathers. These form the outermost covering on the bird and give the creature its shape, impression of size, its colour, texture and character. There is an infinite variety of contour feathers – from the peacock's metre-and-a-half long uppertail coverts, to the microscopic plumes on a hummingbird's eyelid, less than half a millimetre long – but they obey the same simple format.

A hard central hollow shaft divides a feather in half to the tip and each side of it is called a web. Technically that hollow shaft is known as the rachis, but you'll know it as a quill, the object central to our own written communication until we invented the fountain pen. On either side of the rachis is a complex sequence of side branches called barbs. From each of these thousands of barbs on a single feather spreads a secondary network of finer hair-like structures called barbules. The barbules are tipped with interlocking hooklets and these knit the web of a feather tightly together, giving it its overall elasticity and strength. When a bird preens, part of its intention is to reconnect those tiny hooklets on the barbules so that the feathers are literally zipped back into perfect shape.

Contour feathers are not randomly distributed over a bird in a haphazard patchwork. They obey fixed sequences – a number of precisely arranged feather tracts that recur on almost all the world's species. Breaking down a bird into its different constituents is the very basis of birding and in any bird book or field guide the first thing in the introductory text is a series of line drawings of birds covered in little arrows, with words underneath like submoustachial stripe, or supercilium, or greater coverts. The system of names given to these different body parts is known as bird topography.

The use of a geographical term might be coincidental but, fortuitously, it conveys the notion that a single bird is an entire landscape. That annotated illustration with its arrows and bizarre terminology is essentially a map of a birder's world. We live and have our being in that place. I've spent many a happy hour wandering amongst the scapulars on a Herring Gull's back, or dwelling with the primary projection on Lesser Short-toed Larks. You now need to know at least some of the main locations in that world before the story can go much further.

The line of, usually, about twenty large feathers at the rear edge of a bird's wing comprises the main flight feathers, called the primaries and secondaries. The outer eleven are primaries – pinions in layman's terms. There are almost always either ten or eleven attached to the outer wing bone, know as the hand or manus. Individually primaries are asymmetrical in shape. The outer web is almost always narrower in a primary because it has to be stiff and strong to slice through the air. The similar feathers nearer to the body than the primaries are called the secondaries. They're broad and long, more symmetrical in shape and they give the bird uplift in flight. They attach to the bone called the ulna or forearm and their number can vary dramatically from species to species. On a long-winged bird such as an albatross there may be as many as forty. On some species of swift there are just eight.

Overlaying these two main tracts at the front of the wing are three protective bands of feathers called coverts – the greater, median and lesser coverts. When the bird lands the primaries slide beneath the secondaries and all then tuck neatly against the body, and often virtually disappear beneath the coverts and three or four broad, large feathers known as tertials.

Learning and seeing these tracts on the moving bird is a large part of the art of bird recognition. In fact one could say that birding is largely the mastery, not of birds themselves, but their component parts, the feathers. But feathers are not just integral to a bird's identity, they are central to a birder's identity. No birder can be unaware of the existence or whereabouts of the submoustachial stripe or the tertials. You can be a birdwatcher, a bird-lover, a bird-spotter, a robin-stroker, even an ornithologist, but you're not a birder.

I've regularly been down the pub with kindred souls when the main topic of conversation has been the colour of the tertials, or the barring on the tertials, or whether there is a pale fringe on the tertials of a particular species. I'm a birder and even I find it boring, but that's not the point. I know what they're saying. They know what I'm talking about. Our identities are sheltered beneath the umbrella of those tertials. I belong. They belong. But if you don't know about tertials, you don't, and that's the point.

When I saw that Short-eared Owl on Goldsitch Moss I didn't know what or where were the tertials or the submoustachial stripe. I didn't even know much about primaries or secondaries. At that stage I wasn't a birder. But one thing I did know. I was going to be one.

5

Bins and Scope

In the list of debts to those who shaped my first years of birding the oldest of my IOUs is made out to my brother Andy. One Christmas he received a cheap pair of Boots 8x30 binoculars. I'm not sure why he wanted some, but when I took up birds he generously allowed me to use them. I have to confess that I didn't so much borrow as commandeer them. And once I'd started to go out to Lightwood or on the Buxton Field Club outings he never really saw them again. By the time I replaced them I actually thought they were mine.

Not that they were any good. In fact they were useless. Had I used them for much longer I'd probably have suffered permanent eye damage. But *then* I thought they were wonderful and I still remember them clearly and with affection – the chipped black-metal body, the star-burst flaws in the object lenses, the staples that held the leather straps together.

They were the first object of desire in a long relationship with optical technology; an affair that's central to most birders' lives and which borders on a marriage. Currently mine is a neatly bigamous arrangement – the second pair is kept permanently on the desk, while a pair of Leica 8x32s, my first consort as it were, accompanies me wherever I go.

But compared with other birders this promiscuity is modest. Many have the equivalent of an optical harem: pairs for the car, for work, a pair downstairs and maybe one in the bedroom, a little pocketable set for non-birding situations, and several others just in case. Steve Gantlett and Richard Millington, joint editors of *Birding World*, with homes overlooking the legendary reserve at Cley in Norfolk, have telescopes and tripods permanently in place on the landing.

It goes without saying that when you're out birding, you have a pair of binoculars around your neck all day. When you go into a shop or sit down for a drink, or a meal, you'd never dream of taking them off. This physical attachment is more than simply a case of being prepared for the unexpected. Birders sometimes keep them on when they go to conferences or society meetings, or any function where the main focus is birds. Occasionally they actually use them. At slide talks it feels much more like the real thing to line up at the back of the hall, watching the bird images on screen through a pair of 8x40s.

Even more strange, though, is the fact that birders take their binoculars to the Rutland Bird Fair. This is an annual event held over three days and represents the biggest bird jamboree in the world. It takes place at the nature reserve of Rutland Water, but seeing birds is not a high priority. It's a moment when everyone involved in the industry (and I use that word deliberately) – clubs, societies, bird-book sellers, wildlife-holiday companies and, especially, manufacturers of optics – gathers to tout their wares. The exhibitors are there for commercial and possibly social purposes, while the thousands of punters wander through half a dozen huge marquees sampling the fare on several hundred stands. And many do this with the best part of a thousand pounds' worth of optics round their necks. Often they even have a telescope and tripod dangling at their side for good measure.

It looks strange, but it's only inexplicable if the bins and scope (no one really talks about binoculars or telescopes) are presumed to have a practical function. Their true purpose is a statement about identity. It's this, what you might call the psychology of optics, which fascinates me.

★　　★　　★

First we need to consider a few technical details. From their origins in the nineteenth century binoculars have followed the same basic format. They are, in essence, a pair of metal tubes with openings at either end for the light to enter and exit. The larger end, the far end, is known as the objective or object lens and is the part that receives the light from the subject being viewed. The light rays then travel through the tube, bouncing off a sequence of glass prisms before exiting at the ocular, or eyepiece, having been magnified by internal lenses in the process.

In any binoculars a number of factors determines the kind of image produced. First, the size of the object lens controls the amount of light admitted, and of the specifications that attach to any model – 8x30, 8x32, 10x40 – the second number indicates the object lens diameter. The first figure tells you the number of times the image is magnified. Quite simply, a pair of eight times bins means that the subject appears eight times closer. One might think that the highest magnification would be the ideal, but with this there's a trade off since you lose field of view, which is the spatial amount you can actually see in the image. High mag normally means narrow field of view, which is no good when you're searching for small birds in a dense thicket of vegetation.

There's another major consideration when you're choosing bins, which has to do with a thing called the exit pupil. This refers to the shaft of light transmitted from the eyepiece to the observer's eye. The larger the diameter of the exit pupil the brighter the image will appear. This is calculated by dividing the diameter of the object lens by the magnification. So a pair of 8x32s like mine gives you an exit pupil of 4 millimetres. In a pair of 10x50s it would be five. In order to have optimum performance in a range of situations, birders want fairly good magnification, a large field of view and generally an exit pupil of around four or five. That's why the most popular models are 8x32s or 10x40s.

While the principles determining which bins to use have largely remained the same, the quality of the optics has changed out of all recognition. Most of the earlier manufacturers were probably producing them for military or naval purposes and you could tell. They seemed to work on a standard axiom that fighting men needed equipment that measured up to their machismo and if the bins didn't hang round your neck like lead weights they couldn't possibly be decent lenses. Many were shaped like two huge barrels each the length of a small lighthouse. They'd have specifications like 16x60.

Often they had no central focusing mechanism and each eyepiece had to be adjusted independently. I could imagine them in the hands of someone watching the horizon for an enemy aircraft carrier. Or possibly someone scanning from the crow's nest of a whaling vessel. But you could tell they hadn't been designed for spotting leaf warblers flitting through the treetops. Sometimes the image produced was bisected by a pair of hair-line sights, or even a grid of intersecting lines with numbers down the side. Looking through them, you felt you were not so much intended to identify birds as blow them up.

But when I first started – dare I call it the old days? – ancient binoculars carried no stigma. In fact, many people thought old was good. To look weather-beaten, to have a pound of grit on the inside of your object lens, and to have them worn down to pure brass on those parts that were in contact with the body – these were paraded like old battle scars. Like 'my' old Boots 8x30s, these sorts of bins were completely useless, but their perversely loyal owners would hand them to you for examination, boasting they'd recently compared them with a new top model, and there hadn't been much in it. Admittedly most other people did have a few problems focusing. But what did you think?

Then you'd look down and find a dim monochrome scene swimming out of focus behind a fog of scratchmarks, black specks and what looked like green fungus growing on the prisms. You'd hand them back feeling slightly queasy, with some polite comment about them possibly needing a bit of a service.

But if, in the old days, the bins were bad, the scopes were even worse. In the early 1970s most people relied solely on their bins, but if they were serious then they had to make a choice between one of only three new telescope models, the Nickel Supra, the Hertel and Reuss and the Swift Telemaster. The Nickel was dreadful. It was like looking down the cardboard tube from a toilet roll. The Hertel, the scope I eventually bought, was much better. It was like looking through the cardboard tube from a kitchen roll. Like the Nickel, the Hertel was a zoom scope, and you could twist the lens out to increase magnification from twenty-five to sixty times. I used to love sitting in a hide and watching waders at minimum distance with maximum magnification, so that you could see every detail on, say, a Snipe's tertials. You were so close to the beast you felt you knew what it was like to be a feather louse.

I have to confess that optically the best of the three scope options was the Swift Telemaster. The only disadvantage with it was it was so short. In those days you didn't have a tripod to stand it on, as everyone does today. Birders had to either find something to rest it on, usually a friend's shoulder or a fence post; otherwise you had to adopt the standard birder-using-scope position, which was lying on your back, legs crossed with the telescope's object lens balanced on the side of your calf and your spine tilted upwards so you could get your eye to the other end. Unfortunately the Swift Telemaster was so short that that position was a physical impossibility. It's probably why most people either had a Nickel or a Hertel, for all their shortcomings. But even with one of these two, using it while on your back was like achieving one of the postures in Iyengar yoga. Some birders blame a lifetime of back trouble on adopting that position.

There was one way to alleviate the problem and that was to obtain an old brass telescope – the sort that you see ghillies using in ancient photos of people deer-stalking. If you can't imagine one of these, think of Nelson holding a scope to his unseeing eye, then multiply its length by three. The old brass scopes were huge and their original manufacture was probably also for military purposes, but up until the 1970s a brass scope was also a key insignia of a *real* birder. I always lamented that I never had one.

They were difficult to find and not easy to use when you did. A key problem was their weight. When not extended the brass sections concertina-ed together and were snugly housed in leather sockets that were permanently attached to the strap. Unfortunately that solid cylinder of metal weighed a ton. Birders carrying them tended to lean with one scope-burdened shoulder slightly lower than the other. But brass scopes really came into their own when you were lying down, since it was relatively straightforward to rest a three-foot-long pipe on your leg and look out of the other end. However, as the birder and TV comedian Bill Oddie made clear in a wonderful description of his own scope, holding that position for any length of time was no mean feat. 'Can you conceive how excruciatingly agonising that was?' Oddie recalls:

> If not, you might care to try it sometime. If you can't find an old brass scope, a large cucumber will do. And, come to think of it, it will probably be about as effective optically. And don't just do it for a few minutes; stay there for several hours. Then try and get up. I promise you, you'll have a new-found respect for the legendary old seawatchers who used to lie there for days looking at nothing off Selsey Bill. Then again, you might realise that they weren't so much dedicated as stuck. People died in that position and no one realised for months. If you did survive you were left with a posture like the Hunchback of Notre Dame. But we wore our stoop with pride.

The great advantage of these scopes, which Bill Oddie doesn't mention, was their sheer ruggedness. For instance, it could double up as a fantastic weapon. Birders can get into pretty lonely, potentially hazardous, situations. But most people would think twice about taking on someone wielding a three-foot tube of brass. And then there was always the opportunity for do-it-yourself entertainment. There is a wonderful old story of birders on the Isles of Scilly who, when the birds were thin on the ground, had a scope-throwing competition, a birder's equivalent of tossing the caber. The great thing about brass scopes was that there was no loss of quality through such handling. They were always crap.

Massive improvements in optical technology during the last twenty years have had a revolutionising effect on birding, in particular they made that intimate micro-landscape of feathers described in the previous chapter that much more accessible. But they've also done away with some of the old social certainties. A problem that's become more acute is that of identifying the abilities of a birding stranger. There was a time when you could assume that someone possessing good binoculars automatically knew what they were talking about, which was critical when you wanted to know what birds were around. A serious birder, even if he were the most impoverished teenager, would strive to own a pair of Zeiss or Leitz, the two top brands until the 1980s. In fact the depth of contrast between the optics' value and the impoverished appearance of their owner was the best index of ability. Spot a young guy in raggedy old T-shirt, baseball boots, jeans that hadn't been washed for weeks, *plus* a pristine pair of Zeiss 10x40s, and you were clearly on safe ground. It told you that most of that birder's entire worldly wealth was round his neck. Today, unfortunately, expensive binoculars indicate almost nothing. Birding has entered the mainstream of consumer culture. Today you can meet a couple decked out with £3000 worth of optics and it will tell you little of sociological importance, except the ludicrous follies of conspicuous consumption.

But one thing the new range of super-bins has done is intensify further the key experience which *all* optical equipment, however bad, confers on its user – those sensations of liberty and clarity that are so much more difficult to find in ordinary life. If you can't imagine what I'm talking about, then try it. Worried about your job, your relationship, money, sex or how you're going to pay for the £1000 pair of binoculars you've just bought on credit? Then raise them to your eyes, look at those five gulls beating a determined path across the sky, or that small murmuration of starlings swirling above the city, and the problem's on its way to being solved. Or at least it's nowhere to be seen.

Most binoculars allow you about eight degrees of vision. It means that for the moments you hold them to your eyes, the other 352 degrees are completely excluded. Anything within the orbit of those eight degrees is magnified and enhanced, while everything else – job, relationship, money, sex – is consigned to the aura of darkness around you. That, in a nutshell is the joy, the magic, of binoculars. They convert life into something else, something almost abstract, something purer, clearer, usually more beautiful and almost always something you'd never really seen that way before. That's what birders are hooked on – not the physical object, the complex prisms and lenses of binoculars, but their wondrous alchemical power to transform you and your state of being. When I saw those Meadow Pipits grovelling around in fields at Lightwood, or that Short-eared Owl sailing above the moors at Goldsitch Moss it was this new way of seeing, as much as the birds themselves, which transfixed me. And life could never be the same again.

6

The Cave Wall

1 adult Ross's Gull, Rhodostethia rosea
Scalby Mills, Yorkshire, 25 April 1976

Birders are sometimes asked what's their most essential piece of equipment. Given my own particular fetish for notebooks, which I declare right now, I'd like to say that *they* are the most valuable item in the kitbag. Unfortunately they're not.

I said earlier that birding is a triangular relationship between birds, light and observer. The light, that anarchic trembling atmosphere of electromagnetic radiation, is the medium through which birder and bird literally become one, if only momentarily. The light waves that strike the bird and illuminate its surface eventually enter the ganglia on the birder's retina and are converted into a flood of chemical impulses racing to the occipital cortex. In some of our brains' ten thousand million neurons they trigger waves of electro-chemical interactions which we know as emotion, memory, thought.

Those particles of converted light-energy are, in aggregate, our experience of any bird and they persist in the observer's mind until the brain ceases to function or they are erased slowly by dementia. It's at this unseen, mysterious level that birding really has its meaning. Therefore anything that enlarges and intensifies the visual experience has to be the entrance tunnel to the birder's world. Optics are that *key* channel of communication and anyone who argues otherwise is lying or attempting to shock. Bins are definitely a birder's best friend.

So I have to admit that notebooks only achieve second place in the hierarchy of equipment, but they're an important counterpart to binoculars because if optics intensify the birding experience, then notebooks offer a form of release from its inarticulable power. Scribbling down and sketching something about the process of contact between you and the birds are ways of unravelling its meaning.

My own compulsion to keep notebooks began when I was thirteen, since when I've completed forty-six, with three lost. It's driven, I guess, by something like the same impulse that drives art. It's a rush of feelings and thoughts that must somehow be encoded. Although I need to emphasise I make no claims for my notebooks. The drawings, which have barely improved over three decades, are wooden and clumsy, while the writing is often illegible and lacking in original perception. I mean simply that they're products of the same process which results in art. I suspect that even bald, unadorned lists of birds seen on a particular day are often displaced attempts to convey the poetry of the experience.

In fact when I began that was all I found to say about any day in the field: a list of the birds. Then I started adding numbers, which reached a kind of obsessive crescendo just a year later. At its height I'd attempt to count every single individual bird I saw and, intermittently, I'd stop to note them all down. Even this, however, is a mild compulsion compared with leading British birder, Richard Millington, who during his childhood in Hampshire walked round his local patch at Fleet Pond, three, four, possibly five times a day logging down every sparrow, every blackbird, every robin he saw on *each* visit.

Occasionally I came close to Richard's dedication. Between the ages of thirteen and sixteen I used to go regularly with two or three friends and a teacher from our school to a birding location on the Yorkshire coast called Spurn Head. Some pages of my first (surviving) notebook from that period, a tiny page-a-day

diary for 1973, carry just a single species' name surrounded by
columns of individual figures. For instance on the third page
devoted to 23 May there is the word 'Swallow' followed by 128
separate entries of numbers. Altogether these different figures
add up 347 Swallows, the total we saw that day between the
hours of nine-thirty a.m. and two o'clock in the afternoon.
Each separate number signifies a party of Swallows flying past
a migration watchpoint at Spurn known as the 'Narrows'. I
spent hundreds of happy hours standing at that spot, logging
the movements of common migrants.

In a sense the tally of 347 Swallows on 23 May 1973 is a perfect
measure of how intensely personal and utterly worthless most of
the contents of my notebooks really are. However, I did graduate
that year to more penetrating insights into bird behaviour. For
instance on 23 February in my thirteen-year-old's rather fragile,
joined-up writing, there are the words: 'a common gull chased
a redshank which had food in its mouth. The redshank dropped
it and flew off.' A comparably rich nugget follows shortly after:
'a flock of lapwings mobbed a kestrel and a common gull'.

I don't think it matters that what I wrote was pointless.
The key thing was the discipline of committing it to paper.
It developed a note-taking habit that will never leave me,
and I think note-taking has a number of major benefits. First,
it gives you an opportunity as you formulate the narrative,
however rudimentary, to reflect on what you're seeing. More
importantly, it often makes you reflect, as you scribble something
down, on what you omitted to see. This resulting sense of
failure eventually works through to affect the moment of
observation itself. Since you know you're going to write it
later, it concentrates the mind to observe the details you'll want
to recall. In short, it makes you observe more closely.

As they gather, the entries build up a picture of days or weeks
spent in the field. I've only to open an old notebook at what
is for anyone else a half-legible sequence of names and I'm
swimming through the atmosphere of that particular moment.
The list of birds is a memory code for the people with me, the

places visited, the light, the weather, a particular conversation or joke, the taste of salt air in a storm, or the smell of woodland after rain. It is a secret diary on everything that happened that day. In total, the entries are an entire life. And for many like me I suspect they re-awaken the passages of time when we are most intensely alive. It's as a vehicle for the sentimental recovery of these experiences that I most cherish my notebooks.

The other chief impact of accumulating written accounts of your time in the field is that you eventually develop a map of your own past measured out in a grid of dates, locations and significant birds. Most birders have a fairly good recollection of specific good birds. Some, like my Norfolk friend Alan Eardley, have an extraordinarily precise recall of individual sightings, their dates and places stretching back twenty years. If you want to know when the Portland Savannah Sparrow turned up, Alan's your man. I too could give you a rough month-by-month outline of what I was doing and where I was birding for the last twenty-five years. That's nothing special. Most birders can do that. Most, because they take notes.

Sometimes, however, my recall is more specific. I know without reference to any memory aid, for instance, where I was on 19 February or on 5 May 1973. I know that Easter was late in 1973 (Easter Sunday, 23 April), the latest in the last third of a century, because I was birding all that holiday at Spurn Head in Yorkshire. I know I finished my geography O level on 23 June 1976 because that was the day I first hitched to Norfolk to go birding at the coastal reserve of Cley, one of Britain's birding Meccas, which largely determined where I live now.

Measuring life out in lists of bird names is a system that can apply not just to one's personal experience but also to history. I recall, for instance, the day I learnt of Mrs Thatcher's resignation, because I saw her drained tear-swollen face on a huge screen in a restaurant in Khao Yai National Park in Thailand. It was the same day that I first saw Heart-spotted Woodpecker, Indochinese Cuckoo Shrike and Two-barred Greenish Warbler – 23 November 1990. And I know the morning when I heard of

Princess Diana's death, because it's in my notebook as the day I saw three Sabine's Gulls off the coast of Kerry in Ireland. My first, I recall, for twenty-three years.

Although it was several years before I started to add narrative to the plain lists of species, I found ways of highlighting the significance of any experience through a combined system of symbols and different typefaces. A good bird, one I'd seen only a few times in my life, would be written in the notebook in capital letters. A good bird seen well would be in capitals and underlined. A new species would be in block capitals, underlined and have a tick next to it.

By contrast, if we went to look for something rare and didn't find it, then the name of the missed bird would be written down, preceded by the word 'NO' and followed by a series of bold exclamation marks, whose number usually depended on the bird's rarity and the distance we'd travelled. Against that row of lines, ranked like groyne posts on some desolate beach, crashed whole oceans of silent misery. Sometimes it's taken me more than twenty years to cancel that pain by seeing the species in question.

But the notebooks also record comparable moments of joy. A bird in huge block capitals, encircled, with three stars and a tick next to it was an incredible species – something like my first Ross's Gull. This is a rare seabird from the high Arctic (seen only about seventy times in the history of British ornithology; the Scalby bird was about the fifteenth), whose white and pearl-grey plumage is offset in summer by the pink flush on its breast and a necklace of black around the throat. I saw it on 25 April 1976 at Scalby Mills, near Scarborough. It's in notebook six (they're all numbered now).

I open the pages of that flimsy, Baberton Junior jotting pad, held together with sticky tape and staples, and I'm instantly transported to a place ringing with the plangent note of Herring Gulls, to a gathering of fellow birders lying on their backs with scopes fixed on a stretch of rocky shoreline, and a suite of rare birds which had momentarily gathered in one place. In addition to the ROSS'S GULL ★★★, I also wrote down other species warranting capital letters, like MEDITERRANEAN GULL, GLAUCOUS GULL and LITTLE GULL. It is unquestionably one of the red-letter days of my teenage years.

The accumulating significance of my notebooks eventually meant that the physical character of the object itself became increasingly important. Constant daily wear on the kind of soft-covered cash book you find in any stationery shop meant that the thing was often falling apart before you'd even half filled it. In 1977 I looked for something more substantial and lasting and bought my first Alwych notebook, with a robust black laminated cloth 'All-Weather Cover', as it says on the inside front page. Many birders use them and with good reason. They're almost the perfect notebook. Initially I used model A 38/90, with 180 feint-ruled pages. This is seven inches by four and a half, which goes fairly easily into your pocket.

However, in 1982 after seven of these, I graduated with a degree of self-conscious pride to the 280 page A68/140 model. This is eight inches by five. It's a much bigger book, the sort of size that's good for diagrams, for hand-drawn maps, illustrations, multiple sketches with accompanying notes and arrows pointing to important identification criteria. It looks and feels like the notebook of a serious birder. I've used them ever since.

Since 280 pages can accommodate so much text, so many birding records, so many memories from the field, in short, so much of an entire life, a full Alwych becomes an object of huge value. Naturally I became anxious to protect them. The first task when starting each new one is to inscribe my name and address and a guarantee of financial reward were it ever to be lost. Then, as the book fills up almost to completion, I'm confronted with a fresh dilemma. On the one hand there is the uniquely satisfying prospect of adding another completely full Alwych to the pile. On the other hand, there is the nagging thought that I should quit while I'm ahead. Why worry about filling the last twenty pages and run the risk of losing something so priceless?

It's an anxiety other notebook obsessives understand completely. I am deeply grateful to a friend, Richard Campey, not only because he makes my fixation seem relatively normal, but because his solution to such a problem points the way ahead. After several birding trips to Thailand, Richard was planning another visit and wanted to enjoy the comforting familiarity and guidance of his old notes, but didn't dare expose them to the unforeseen danger of a fresh journey. His answer was to photocopy all the memoirs from his previous Thai visits and paste them into the new, as yet, untouched notebook. There was almost no room to write anything fresh, but at least the old volumes were safe and sound on their shelf at home.

Another fellow Alwych fanatic is Richard Porter, former head of species protection at the RSPB. His collection of the little black books holds, as far as we know, the all-comers record: 62 mainly A68/140s and 63 of the smallest A618/80s; almost an entire life – half a century of birding – in 125 volumes. But he, more than most of us, has had to confront a painful truth in his relationship with Alwych.

The notebooks, sadly, are not what they used to be. We have all lamented a decline in the quality of those once indestructible covers, to the point where some question whether Alwych can truly maintain the all-weather legend. Another problem I noted some years ago was the fact that the books were becoming increasingly difficult to find in the shops. In fact, I was so nervous they might stop manufacturing them that in 1990 I bought ten. I still have two completely blank notebooks left on my shelf, enough for about three years' worth of notes . . . just in case.

Yet I must also confess to a touch of adultery regarding my own affair with the beloved Alwych. The sheer size of those crisp white sheets, which is the beauty of the beast, is also their main drawback. Take a tape measure to your pocket. You won't find many that accommodate eight inches by five. I tried to circumvent the problem by always having a little shoulder bag, which developed into an ancillary fetish of its own. But to keep to the point, the Alwych places additional disciplines upon its user. Sometimes it's easier just to leave the notebook at home and do it all from memory when you get back.

Like a monastic order attempting to recover the vigour of its original creed, I searched for an alternative method of keeping notes about three years ago. Then I discovered the policeman's little black notebooks with the elastic-band place marker. They've been a revelation. Four inches long, they fit in any pocket. I carry them everywhere. In an attempt to keep faith with the old order, I find myself writing notes twice: once in the field in a little policeman's pad, then again into the A68/140 when I get home.

I try to tell myself I'd never be unfaithful to the Alwych, lined up in ranks across the special *notebook* shelf, but secretly I love the new books. They carry the thrill of a clandestine relationship. They're so accommodating. They fit so snugly. They are there to hand exactly when you need them. (I also notice that they're rather difficult to find, and in order to pre-empt possible shortage, I scoured the stationers and bought six extras . . . just in case.)

But let's talk now about someone else's notebooks. Because along with a fetish for my own, I have to confess to a secondary obsession with looking at other peoples' notebooks. Though I now get fewer opportunities to indulge it, I've always relished the vicarious thrill of sneaking a glimpse into another's birding experience. Nothing made me more painfully aware of the inadequacy of my own note-taking than rummaging through the notebooks of one of my oldest friends, Richard Grimmett.

His personal library is stacked with filled Alwych A68/140s. In fact if I probed more ruthlessly into my own past I'd probably find it was a subconscious desire to emulate *his* achievements that made me switch to this model myself. Unlike me, though, Richard is a top birder and his notebooks have an unassailable authenticity, to which I'll return.

Richard and I became friends in 1977. He first came to my

attention a year earlier, when he was recognised as one of the hottest young birders on the south coast. He was sixteen and finding a host of good birds near his Sussex home in Rustington. Finding rarities is one of the key measures of ability and Richard shot straight into the birding charts, as it were, when he discovered a Greenish Warbler, close to the rubbish dump on St Mary's, the main island of the Scillies. When he came upon the bird it was already late in the day and it was only the next morning that others, including myself, got to see it.

A Greenish Warbler is a member of the genus *Phylloscopus* and comes to Britain from no nearer than eastern Scandinavia. It's separated from its common British relatives, such as the Willow Warbler and Chiffchaff, by subtle differences in the shade of olive green, structure and the configuration of pale lines across its plumage. Richard acknowledges that waiting for 'his' Greenish to be confirmed was one of the longest nights of his life.

But of course it was a Greenish and proof of early talent. In fact he's one of the best birders I know. Excellent eyesight is one gift. Another is speed. Usually he can get his bins to his eyes before I've even raised mine off my chest. A third gift is artistic ability. It must be more than a coincidence that many top birders are also accomplished draughtsmen. The facility to reproduce on the page what you have seen in the field implies a fuller mental grasp of both the birds' plumage details and the whole process of identification.

Richard's notebooks are full of little pencil sketches. A career in bird conservation has forced him to neglect the craft. But even a small body of work is testament to his ability to re-create birds that appear intensely alive. His first published line drawings, in *A Guide to the Birds of Nepal*, are probably his best. They look so vital it's as if you disturbed them when you opened the book at that page and any second now they're going to fly away.

Yet more than these published vignettes I love the rough sketches in his Alwych notebooks. It's nothing really to do with their artistic merit. It's their contingent quality, their relationship to the moment in the field. The drawings are interwoven with screeds of minute writing on field character, shape, posture, behaviour, habitat, location. Or there might be a gem of a sketch but surrounded by a thicket of false starts, which have been crossed out or abandoned before these birds could even take shape. On the facing page might be a squashed insect, a congealed pool of spilt Coca-Cola, a little calculation in rupees, the maths from that day's dinner bill. Notebooks at their best, conveying not just the birds, but their living context.

Occasionally, although Richard could never have known at the time, his notebooks have almost become valuable documents. A classic example is a series written in the north-eastern states of India, including Assam and Meghalaya, which he visited during a ten-month trip in 1978–9. Richard was eighteen. Hardly any other Western birders have been there since. Those raw notes were later converted into *The Birds of the Indian Subcontinent*, written by Richard with Tim and Carol Inskipp, a 900-page tome and amongst the ten most important bird field guides in the last quarter of the twentieth century.

Whenever I think seriously about *why* I love notebooks I'm reminded of those cave walls covered in drawings of game by our Neolithic ancestors. Bison, deer and horses gallop across their subterranean galleries in exuberant patterns of charcoal and ochre. These paintings – perhaps never intended for anyone's eyes except their creators and then entombed in darkness for thousands of years – strike me as a comparable attempt by someone to wrest their own private meaning from the hunting experience. They are also provisional statements by a mind filled, possibly overwhelmed, by the sheer magic of a long hard day in the field. They are precious documents about our past, but also about our present condition, since their unconscious beauty finds its echo – if not a direct lineal descendant – in the birder's notebook.

To think that on a birder's death some notebooks end up on a bonfire of 'unwanted' personal effects, lit by surviving relatives who fail to grasp their larger significance, is a real tragedy. There ought to be a section in a national library or museum dedicated solely to birding culture, where the notebooks of all great naturalists can be gathered once their authors have passed away. If you were ever in need of inspiration to get back out in the field, you could flick through a few dozen, revelling in the insights and the frozen moments of joy from nature. But when you go along, keep a look out for the old requisition slips. Some of them are bound to have my name on.

7

Roger Tory Peterson's Oystercatcher

1 adult Iceland Gull, Larus glaucoides
New Brighton, 10 March 1974

Many leisure activities have helped define, and have themselves been shaped by, our sense of social hierarchy in Britain. But birding now lies almost totally outside that territory. Unlike golf, say, or sailing and cricket, which are still partly bound up with the class system, in the world of birds the issue almost never raises its ugly head. During my own thirty years I've come across almost nothing that could be defined as a matter of class. That's because almost all birders come from much the same broad social background – the working and middle classes. In fact I can think of only about three active birders with double-barrel surnames.

That wasn't the case forty years ago. In 1959, the year I was born, the birding hierarchy was from the same social stratum that held sway in most departments of cultural life. Look in that year's centenary issue of *The Ibis,* the journal of the British Ornithologists' Union, and you'll see its council included a wing-commander, a professor of modern languages at Edinburgh and a Fellow of the Royal Society. Its president was a Cambridge don, the secretary was an old Etonian and a senior editor at the publisher, Collins, James Fisher. Its vice-presidents included the distinguished senior civil servant, Max Nicholson, who had been with Churchill at Yalta in 1944.

Even this represented a slight widening of ornithology's social borders. Earlier in the century it was the domain of millionaire bankers, famous explorers, the sons of famous explorers and millionaire bankers, the officer classes, landed gentry and the odd country vicar.

Since then birding has made a long, seemingly irreversible journey down the social ladder. There's a famous anecdote from the 1950s involving the legendary American bird artist, Roger Tory Peterson. He'd gone with a mixed party of birding bigwigs to Hilbre, the small island in the Dee estuary, to look at the gathering flocks of waders. After the excursion, Lord Alanbrooke, keen birder and Chief of Imperial General Staff during the Second World War, was expanding on his relations with Sir Winston Churchill. But in the midst of the Field-Marshal's historical monologue, Tory Peterson turned to the group and said, 'I guess Oystercatchers will eat most any kind of mollusc.'

It's been the prevailing attitude ever since. Birders like to stick to life's main source of interest. If you're sufficiently enthusiastic about animals with feathers then that's all that really matters. Derek Moore, director of conservation at the Wildlife Trusts, recalls bird outings that featured a heterogeneous social quartet: a GP, an accountant, himself and a punk rocker. The Sex Pistols fan was the nicest, quietest fellow you could imagine, but the intimidating mix of safety pins and fluorescent mohican were great for getting rapid service at the bar.

Just because we don't care about social class doesn't mean birding is free of division. In fact birding is as hierarchical as any other activity in the country, it's just the issues that separate one group from another are entirely bound up within the tribe itself. Anybody outside it could blunder through the taboos, snapping gossamer-fine conventions like spider's webs, so I've prepared a small anthropological paper to help you find your way around.

Most bird people would probably tell you that there are roughly eight sub-clans in the tribe – scientist, ornithologist, bird-watcher, birdwatcher, birder, twitcher, dude and robin stroker. Almost everyone would see themselves as belonging to one of only four of these eight categories. The other four are names for tiny minorities or are used by one set of bird people for another.

Let's take them in batches. 'Ornithologist' and 'scientist' overlap pretty much completely. They refer to those people who have done a PhD on birds, or are supervising others doing a PhD on birds. Even they would rarely classify themselves as an 'ornithologist'. But even if they don't, a great sadness of modern bird culture is that serious academic ornithology has lost its mooring amongst the legions of gifted amateurs. The old spiritual home of the latter, the British Ornithologists' Union, for a hundred years *the* central national institution, has drifted steadily further away from the general community, losing membership and tribal relevance as it does so.

Its quarterly journal, *The Ibis*, one of the oldest ornithological publications in the world, is still a place where serious bird science can be published, and rightly so; but few ordinary birders take it. Those who do privately admit that they seldom read it and I openly confess I can't understand it. It has papers with titles like 'Effects of density-dependence and weather on population changes of English passerines using a non-experimental paradigm', or 'Provisioning and growth rates of nesting Fulmars *Fulmarus glacialis*: stochastic variation or regulation?' Then there's the old potboiler, 'Cost reduction in the cold: heat generated by terrestrial locomotion partly substitutes for thermoregulation costs in Knot *Calidris canutus*'. And who could possibly resist that old love-triangle, 'Extra-pair paternity in the socially monogamous Sedge Warbler *Acrocephalus schoenobaenus* as revealed by multilocus DNA fingerprinting'?

The word for the American Indian tribe, the Apache, was derived from a Zuni expression meaning 'the enemy'. Dude and robin-stroker, are in the same class of name. They're clearly pejorative terms and no one in their right mind would call themselves either. A robin-stroker is the easier to define. They are the most lukewarm in their enthusiasm. Like my parents, they heap food on the bird table. They watch from the living-room window. They join the Royal Society for the Protection of Birds and, instead of a leading-edge conservation outfit, they often think they're supporting an organisation devoted to injured creatures. Despite the implied slur of sentimentality, robin-strokers are the vast bulk of decent folk without whom bird conservation would have no real teeth. We should all learn to love and stroke them fondly.

The dude is a more complex stereotype. His central feature is ignorance, or rather, you should put this the other way round. His perceived deficiency is expertise. When used in this specific sense, and it sometimes is, it's an unacceptable insult for someone less experienced than ourselves. Let's face it, we were all dudes once. But 'dude' also carries a vague moral implication, suggesting a person who purports to know things they patently don't. A dude is the most unwelcome character in any rigid hierarchy – the person with pretensions above his station. Just like 'robin-stroker', the use of the word is indefensible, but we need to acknowledge that the term and the category exist. I admit with shame that many birders use it regularly, including myself.

The third batch – bird-watcher, birdwatcher, birder and twitcher – is the part of the tribe to which almost all of us belong. I list birdwatcher and the ridiculously hyphenated bird-watcher separately only in a bid to banish the latter for ever. Even as a single word, 'birdwatcher' sounds so passive and voyeuristic that you'd probably be far more disinclined to take it up. But if you need to stick a hyphen between the two words you've obviously *never* been involved in the enterprise in your life. No member of the bird tribe should ever use it. So let's proscribe it now. As for those who dare to present it as two words, bird watcher, they ought to face legal action.

Now we come to the last two. James Fisher was the familiar, official BBC voice on most bird matters until he crashed his Jag on the M1 in 1970. Fisher was using the far more dynamic 'birding' by the early 1960s. For me the verbs 'to bird' or 'to go birding' suggest the appropriate depth of identification between observer and his subject. Surely that's why it's taken such a firm subconscious root in the tribal patois? Although it's not completely accepted in bird literature; editors of journals and magazines still feel the more formal 'birdwatcher' is a safer bet. There are also even a few senior warriors who cling to the old ways. Ian Wallace, whose initials DIMW are probably the most reproduced four letters in modern British bird literature, still hankers for a vanished tribal unity of purposeful observers and insists on calling them and himself 'birdwatchers'. But the tide's against him. This is a birders' world. I suspect 90 per cent of active bird people would use the form both as noun and verb.

It's only competitor is 'twitcher' and here we come to the really meaty topic – one could almost call it a class issue – in the world of birds. Rather like the term 'bird-watcher', twitcher is probably used more by non-bird people than birders themselves. But whereas bird-watcher betrays simple ignorance, people use 'twitcher' to suggest they're really up on your subject. The usual question, 'Oh you're one of these *twitchers*, are you?' is supposed to be proof of some kind of wildlife street cred. To most of us it's simply irritating, but it's useful to this extent: I now have to explain the word, the activity and the debate that lies behind it.

Put at its most simple, twitching is the pursuit of rare birds. It can involve long-distance travel, but that isn't a defining characteristic. I regularly go twitching in Norfolk and it seldom involves more than a forty-mile journey. It would be wrong to suggest absolutely everybody does it, but I would like to meet the keen birder who claims never to have done so. We all like to see rarities. As in any other activity which involves collecting it's a central part of the pursuit. We wouldn't expect philatelists to spend all their energies collecting more and more of the same brown 26-pence first-class stamps. They want one with the queen's head the wrong way round, or with Elizabeth sporting a moustache or George VI's beard. Collectors enjoy the rare, the unusual, the anomalous, the quirky, the erroneous. Birders are the same.

But twitching has often been given the character of an extremist activity and carries all sorts of negative connotations. It's seen in some quarters as fanatical, self-indulgent, thoughtless, uncaring, competitive, frivolous and, despite being rooted in an obsession with natural history, as actually anti-environmental. Those defined as twitchers are sometimes heaped with the kind of odium which the above vices usually elicit and I need to disentangle the more complex truth from a vast pile of misunderstandings.

I have to confess that my own bird apprenticeship took place in a milieu where the twitcher was seen as about the most evil creature alive. Spurn Head Bird Observatory on the Yorkshire coast is a wonderful location to start birding. A slender four-mile-long finger of sand dune sticking into the North Sea, Spurn was identified long ago as a perfect spot to witness bird migration. Birds travelling south along the coast are forced to follow this fragile isthmus until it is extinguished in the swirling currents of the North Sea. A classic example was the Swallows we counted as they streamed past us on 23 May 1973. At the 'Narrows', Spurn Point is no more than a few yards wide. It is the key strategic spot – one of the best in Britain – to intercept birds on their spring and autumn passage.

Although I owe a huge debt to its community of birders, many of those who went regularly to Spurn saw themselves as a kind of antithesis to the twitcher. We were involved in a form of birding that added to the sum of 'ornithological knowledge' (to be enunciated in reverential tones). It was scientific and purposeful. Although quite what purpose there was in noting down 347 Swallows heading south between the hours of nine-thirty a.m. and two p.m. on 23 May 1973 seems a little more unclear now than it did at the time.

But it was a sober, virtuous pastime. It was not for us – the notion of haring off after rarities. We earned them. We stayed put. We stood at the Narrows for days on end, waiting, hoping, for something unusual. And when it came, such as the gorgeous little Red-footed Falcons from eastern Europe that graced Spurn that late sunlit spring, we had a feeling of propriety about them. This was our local patch and those rarities were *ours* too. Anybody steaming in from London or Manchester would have been looked upon as thieves stealing our deserved good fortune.

However, there is nothing quite like sampling a vice to change your notions of virtue. I have to confess that even as we absorbed the moral strictures of the Spurn Head community, twitching had come to acquire something of the lustre of all forbidden fruit. Just nine months after those Red-footed Falcons, by the beginning of notebook two, I was happy to risk my ornitho-virginity.

Needless to say, I remember it well. It was 10 March 1974. I was fourteen. She – so to speak – was eighteen. Or rather, I should say, that this particular bird, an Iceland Gull, had been coming to the same sewage outflow pipe at New Brighton on the Wirral for eighteen consecutive winters. It was not just a twitch, I was buying into a piece of birding history. Hundreds, probably thousands, of birders active from the 1960s onwards saw that particular bird at one time or another.

It was a beautiful creature. It differs from the common-or-garden Herring Gull, the bird whose gales of manic laughter can be heard as you eat your seaside fish and chips, by subtle differences in wing pattern. Adult Herring Gulls have black tips enclosing white spots, known as mirrors, at the very wing end. The Iceland has white tips to pearl grey wings. Out of habit you look every time to ensure the ordinariness of a Herring Gull's identity. But to check one time and find that the tips were not those of a Herring Gull and then to take in the other fine differences of this scarce and lovely gull – its dovelike head, its gentler mien, its long wings and effortless buoyancy – was a fantastic thrill.

To me it looked preternaturally pale and seeing this ghostly bird for the first time bordered on the orgasmic. It's another reason why I question the old birder's I-birdwatch-because-I-can't-botanise-in-winter argument. Look away now if you're squeamish, but I well remember a Barnsley birder in irresistible South-Yorkshire tones, announcing after seeing one particular rarity, 'It were so good I nearly creamed me pants.' That robust male directness gets to the nub of the matter. Birds can be erotic. (Surely that's why half the male population in Britain still refer to women as *birds*? And it's not just the English. The popular German word for sex is *vögeln*, 'to bird'. The Italian word for 'bird', *l'ucello*, is also a 'penis', which is a close parallel to our own slang 'cock'.)

But the key revelation from twitching that wonderful Iceland Gull on 10 March 1974 wasn't its eroticism. It was the sheer innocence of it. That's where all twitching starts: that pure uncontaminated joy in seeing something beautiful and rare. In fact, if you trace the word 'twitching' to its etymological roots, you find a story so heart-warming, so innocent, so homely, it's hard to believe its devotees have come to represent the ornithological Dark Side.

The word began life as part of the banter between a quartet of good friends, including Bob Emmett and Howard Medhurst, now venerable elder statesmen of Britain's birding scene. In the late 1950s Howard had been elected to Britain's first rarities committee, a council of ten top birders who adjudicate records of rare birds submitted by their peers. Part of his self-appointed task was to go and check on good birds seen within striking distance of London, a journey he generally covered on the pillion of Bob Emmett's Matchless 350. The couple on the other motorbike enjoyed the creature comforts, as Emmett himself has written, of Jan, 'a back-warming, lap-warming dog' who, squeezed between pillion and rider, ensured that all three arrived in fine shape. Unfortunately the pillion of the Matchless had no comparable heating facilities and after a long journey in all weathers, Howard Medhust arrived frozen to the bone.

His natural response was to shiver uncontrollably, while his instinct was to reach for a Woodbine and enjoy the soothing warmth of its smouldering coal. Added to this was their collective excitement as they anticipated the rare bird they'd all come to see. The pattern recurred wherever they went, and the other three eventually made it a standard joke to re-enact Howard's trembling performance. A birding trip thus became known as 'being on a twitch' and the phrase caught on. When Howard, an employee of British Petroleum, returned in the mid-1960s from a stint abroad, he found 'twitching' was part of the vernacular. Now it's in the *Oxford English Dictionary* and Britain's prototype-twitcher has been embarrassed ever since.

It's not surprising. Forty years later the word still carries a taint of disapproval. Although, strangely enough, the media's constant misapplication of the twitcher label to just about everyone interested in birds has to some extent diluted its dishonourable associations. Yet at one time every kind of vilification was heaped on the word and those it appeared to name. There have been high-profile incidents – I'll describe some shortly – in which twitchers acquired a bad name. But like all incidents that attract attention, it's the worst that linger longest. People forget the countless occasions when nothing newsworthy happens, when there are no fences broken, no farmers offended or abused, no muck-spreaders deployed in anger, no tempers lost or notoriety established.

The twitcher's reputation probably reached its nadir in the early 1980s, and the incident that best illustrates the prevailing climate involved the publication of a book, which was subtitled *The Birdwatching Year of Richard Millington*. The year in question was 1980 while Richard – he of Fleet Pond regularity – was an up-and-coming bird illustrator and twitcher, and now a leading figure in the birding world. His experiences during that particular twelve-month period are presented as a series of journal entries listing the dates, locations and birds he saw, together with brief personal comments and details.

It's written in a fast-paced conversational style. It has no pretensions to literariness and it was largely a vehicle for Richard's characteristic sketches and paintings. But the text captures accurately and in unselfconscious fashion, the behaviour, lifestyle, linguistics and obsessions of a top birder. One notable sighting, for instance, is commemorated with the words: 'Scored at last'. He describes another bird, a Sooty Tern, as 'a total blocker', while of a third species, a Steller's Eider, he writes, 'Finally unblocked this one.' But my favourite entry runs: 'This is how twitching should be – the bird safely U.T.B. before breakfast.' What's U.T.B.? Under The Belt, of course!

The Royal Society for the Protection of Birds was so sensitive to public perceptions of birdwatching that when Richard's book appeared as part of a 'Four Books at 99 Pence' style advert for a wildlife book club, the editors thought it best to censor the main title with a bold black strip when the advert appeared in their magazine. For all anybody knew this could have been a scandalous porn book masquerading as bird literature. What were the words we were not to allowed to read? Perhaps *Shagging – A Cormorant-watcher's Guide to Outdoor Sex*? Or possibly beneath his lovely cover illustration of a Scop's Owl, Richard had doodled in a pair of enormous breasts . . . or worse.

But no! The words we were forbidden to see were *A Twitcher's Diary*. I am a massive fan of the RSPB, but this quaint – no, let's be honest, completely insane – piece of corporate prudery has to be recorded for posterity.

This wasn't Richard's only attempt to rehabilitate the word and the activity. A few years later he and Steve Gantlett launched a new birder's publication under the name *Twitching*. But this was equally fraught with complications and the journal only really caught on when it reappeared with its current successful title, *Birding World*. The truth was, and, in fact, still is, even some twitchers don't like to think of themselves as such.

There's a famous description by Bill Oddie in his *Little Black Bird Book* of the twitcher's character. He wrote, 'Bird-watchers [Bill! How could you?] are tense, competitive, selfish, shifty, dishonest, distrusting, boorish, arrogant, pedantic, unsentimental and above all envious.' He was obviously exaggerating for comic effect, and while the description was intended to encompass all birders, it mainly describes the dominant aspect of twitching –

its one-up-manship. But for me, this doesn't describe even a twitcher. It describes just about anyone intensely committed to a narrow field of endeavour. It could be aimed at the Cambridge don when he sees the great reviews for his colleague's little treatise on the metric structure of Catullus' love poetry. It describes the golf club captain when the vice-captain achieves a handicap better than his own. Or the middle-aged male teacher who's just seen his younger female colleague scoop the head of department post. Let's face it, the frailties are human. Twitchers are no more guilty of them than anyone else.

The main issue it raises is this: who are the nasty selfish stereotypical twitchers? If it's anyone, surely, it must be those who have the biggest lists, the people who have seen over 450 or even 500 species in Britain. But hang on. They don't need to go tear-arsing around the country looking for new birds every few days. They've actually seen most of the rare birds that there are to see. At most they'll make five to ten outings a year and probably more like four or five long-distance trips. The truth is that any keen birder who goes twitching spends only a portion of their time chasing rarities. I think it's much more helpful to see twitching as an activity, rather than to go on talking of the twitcher as a distinct category of birder or, even worse, using it as a synonym for all birders.

There is a hard core whom the extremist stereotype might fit more closely. Occasionally they might stray. But we're talking about individuals here, not vast swatches of the community. Most of the time people who twitch are doing what all bird people do: watching their local patch, sending their records into the county recorder, or the national rarities committee, or some BTO (British Trust for Ornithology) record scheme, or writing articles on identification, or little notes on behaviour for *British Birds*, or papers on the faunal limits of the Palearctic, sitting voluntarily on committees of bird clubs and societies, or updating some membership database, or rattling the money box for a conservation charity. In fact many of them are also professionals, working for conservation organisations like the RSPB, English Nature or BirdLife International.

My hope is that there will come a day when the birding tribe is not divided up into little sub-clans, least of all by ourselves. Nor should we hunker down in narrow little shells, peering disdainfully at the neighbours for small differences of approach. Birders should be seen, and should view themselves, as heterogeneous, pluralist and multi-faceted. In my book we should all be fair game for Roger Tory Peterson's famous Oystercatcher at Hilbre – a beast that eats most any kind of mollusc.

8

Where Are You Going, Mate?

1 adult male Steller's Eider, Polysticta stelleri
Vorran Island, Outer Hebrides, 10 July 1976

1976 was the *annus mirabilis* of my twitching period. Even now it's one of the five or six most memorable years of my life and one of those periods when everything clicked. The thrill of seeing rare birds was established but until 1976 the opportunity had been lacking, or lacking on a regular basis. Now I teamed up with a group of keen birders from Buxton and our luck held for a whole twelve months.

It began with a day trip to the wooded valleys of central Wales, which were then a refuge for Britain's only Red Kites. It's strange to think that these birds had once been so widespread and abundant that they'd formed an army of avian scavengers helping to keep the Elizabethan city streets clear of refuse. To me, however, seeing them for the first time as they drifted over the dark oak woods around Devil's Bridge in Dyfed, they seemed better suited to their late-twentieth-century role as icons of Celtic wilderness.

Their long-winged, long-tailed elegance was in striking contrast to the Red-billed Chough, which we saw later that day at the coastal hamlet of Llangranog. High above us we could hear their explosive *K-k-k-yeow* calls, as they lolloped and planed in swirls, moving like wind-blown rags in a gale.

A fortnight later we made a day trip to Norfolk and Suffolk

for Britain's only regular flock of Bean Geese – another new bird. In March it was a second rare goose, a Lesser Whitefront on the Dumbles at Slimbridge in Gloucestershire. The following weekend we were back in Wales for Black-necked Grebes at Llanfairfechan, and a week later for an American vagrant duck called Surf Scoter at Blackpill Harbour near Swansea. An anomalous rarity for Cheshire, a Little Bunting from eastern Scandinavia, separated two spring visits to Yorkshire, first for a charismatic raptor from the far north, a Rough-legged Buzzard, and second for that mythic Arctic inhabitant, the encircled, double-underlined Ross's Gull near Scarborough.

Later in the summer I made two trips to Scotland for some of the specialities of the Highlands: Peregrine, Osprey, Corncrake and Golden Eagle. Seeing these scarce birds in Britain's most beautiful scenery was reward enough, but our real target during the second trip was an extraordinary creature which had been recorded just eight times in this country and the rarest bird I'd ever tried to see. Usually such birds are visitors that stop for a matter of days before moving on. That unpredictable behaviour imposes a major discipline on birders: the need for instant mobility. But the Steller's Eider – the *same* Steller's Eider which Richard Millington had described in his *Twitcher's Diary* as 'finally unblocked' – had been there since 1972. When Richard saw and *unblocked* it, the creature had been in residence for eight years. Altogether it stayed for thirteen. With this rarity time wasn't an issue. It was distance. The bird was near Vorran Island, a pinprick off the west coast of South Uist in the Outer Hebrides. From Buxton it was a cool 1100-mile round trip.

Our means of getting there was a white Saab belonging to Paul Flint. Paul was another Buxton birder and a fanatical twitcher. His British list is now well over 500, one of the top ten in the country and the highest in northern England. He also runs Birdnet, one of the two pager services in the UK providing rare-bird information for birders. By the time I met Paul, his various adventures had already hardened into a series of legends.

Marooned in Buxton, he was always desperate for any form of transport and in his youth regularly rode a Lambretta 125 (45mph max) the 170 miles from Derbyshire to Norfolk. In the absence of his own wheels he'd also hitch. But my favourite story concerned the occasion he walked overnight from Cley in Norfolk to Minsmere in Suffolk. During the early hours of the morning when he'd tramped most of the 60 miles and his feet were bleeding, a police car took pity and drove him the short distance to the RSPB reserve. Captain Flint was just in time to see his first Broad-billed Sandpiper.

That was our nickname for Paul. To myself and two schoolfriends it seemed to capture the immovable sense of purpose written in his face. He's one of those striking examples in which the real name perfectly reflects the personality. There is an adamantine streak in Paul. At its worst, if he were frustrated (when he'd missed the rare bird he'd travelled hundreds of miles to see), it used to plunge him into a kind of moody darkness. At its best, it made him – for us at least – heroic.

He cringes to think it, but we were in awe of his exploits and his driven spirit. In 1976 the daemon had gathered behind a single purpose. He wanted to be the first birder in Britain to see 300 species in a year. He justified it to us and to himself – since it was expensive and time-consuming and eventually cost him his job and his marriage – by suggesting it was the birding equivalent of the sub-four-minute mile. The trip to the Outer Hebrides for Steller's Eider, a bird Paul had already seen himself three years earlier, was part of that larger goal and we weren't complaining. On the contrary. It would be true to say we were intoxicated by a sense of adventure.

And it was not just seeing the birds, wonderful though they were. Twitchers occasionally justify their obsessional pursuit of rarities as one of the best excuses to see the whole of Britain and its offshore islands from end to end. They mean it. I know of no other community which knows and understands better how this vast, dense and infinitely complex country of ours concertinas down into that tiny little archipelago you see on the world map. Twitching enables you to encompass that massive diversity. One moment the acid darkness of the Derbyshire moors, a few hours later the dawn sun is glinting off the shoals of pebbles on a Norfolk beach. You start the day birding among the mist-enfolded marshes near the Dorset coast and by evening you're on Teesside before a rose-tinted industrial landscape reminiscent of a scene from *Star Wars*.

Nor was it simply the kaleidoscope pattern of landscapes that gripped us on that Hebrides trip. You have to remember I was sixteen. Convention dictates to any teenager, in fact, to most normal people that you don't simply set off to drive through the night for 550 miles. You stay put, you go to your mate's house that night, you watch TV and go to bed at ten. You visit the Outer Hebrides perhaps once in your life on a family holiday.

Twitching shatters those restraints. It tells you that you can actually go anywhere at any time. More important, perhaps, is the fact that, on most occasions, when you get there you'll meet scores of others who have made exactly the same journey, reinforcing a communal notion that it's all perfectly normal.

By the time we were north of Glasgow the sun had set. Huddled down in the back of the car, we felt the world contract steadily and any definite sense of location ebbed away with the failing light. Intermittently, the orange flare of the sodium lamps struck us in rhythmic waves and with Captain Flint at the helm, our drive through the Scottish landscape was reduced by darkness to the anonymity of a sea voyage. Lying in the muffled stillness of coat hoods, adrift on teenage thoughts and memories, aware at intervals of the fresh tang of the west coast air, we were filled with a larger, more profound sense of movement – the journey, perhaps, out of adolescence and its framework of dependency.

The journey to the Steller's Eider was my first really long-distance drive for a rare bird. But there was still another, more important rite of passage to face in 1976 in order to be fully a part of the birding tribe. It was to hitch myself. Paul was a veteran. Most young twitchers were. My career began on 23 June 1976.

That particular journey was more than a single rite of passage. It was, in fact, several rolled into one which helped shaped my entire future. It was nothing to do with the geography exam, the last of my O levels, which I sat the same morning. It was because once I'd rushed home and packed a rucksack, I set off for the north Norfolk coast for the first time in my life. I eventually fell under the spell of this magical landscape, still one of my favourites in all the world, and two years later it seemed perfectly logical, when I had to choose a degree course, to opt for English at the University of East Anglia.

But let's be clear. I went there, not because the English department had a reputation, nor because they'd offered me two Cs, or I liked the look of the course; it had even less to do with the televised version of Malcolm Bradbury's *History Man*, which had given the UEA a certain hip notoriety. The exact reason I went to Norwich was Cley, the most famous, arguably the most hallowed, birding location on mainland Britain.

That's where we were heading the warm June afternoon in 1976. My companion was John Mycock, known to me simply as Tog (he has ginger hair and somehow this linked him in child-hood with the red squirrel from the kids' programme, *Pogle's Wood*). Odd, perhaps, and for Tog, occasionally embarrassing, but to me he was always Tog. He still is. We've known each other since he was seven and I was six. I normally introduce him as 'my oldest friend . . . *and* my oldest rival'. Our relationship was a classic teenage sparring match expressed in terms of birds and bird sightings. To some extent it still is. All the time I spent counting swallows at Spurn's Narrow Neck, Tog had been there with me. He was there when I saw the Steller's Eider in the Outer Hebrides. He *wasn't* there when *I* saw the Ross's Gull at Scalby Mills. It was one of many reasons we were rivals.

Two young male teenagers burdened with heavy rucksacks,

complete with tent, cooking pots and dangling boots, we were not the most attractive combination to hitch a lift. The process quickly proved more difficult and less heroic than we'd initially imagined. Several hours later we were still only outside Ashford, just ten miles from Buxton. The temperature was around the ninety mark — the start, in fact, of that famous lifelong summer of sunshine of 1976 — and all through the sweltering afternoon we inched slowly forward. Towards sundown, marooned somewhere in the middle of Lincolnshire, we watched a vast fenland skyscape turn from orange to plum and finally damson. Then the stars came out. The towns we'd passed — Chesterfield, Mansfield, Newark, Sleaford — eventually became a familiar litany in a routine run between Buxton and university. But on that evening we ran out of steam and decided to stop for the night.

We clearly had much still to learn about hitching. In fact we eventually realised it was not just a simple case of standing by the roadside with a thumb out. It was a delicate art with many subtleties and it required tactics. You learnt to stand at some strategic point, by a roundabout or the exit to motorway services, or anywhere the motorists had automatically to slow down. Then there needed be a place for the car to pull in, ahead of where you stood. It was no good causing a multiple-car pile-up. Your lift had to be able to stop safely. Another essential, as well as relatively smart dress, was a sign. And a sign that said PLEASE in block capitals after the destination. It showed you were polite, while the sign itself weeded out people going two miles down the road, whose lift only uprooted you from that strategically chosen spot.

A very handy hitching device was a female friend you could persuade to go to the same destination. It signalled to the potential lift: non-aggressive couple, safe to stop. Although it didn't always work. Once, after we'd been standing two hours without luck, the female friend broke down sobbing uncontrollably, convinced we'd be marooned for ever on that particular stretch of road out of Leicester.

A further trick, one that I never really mastered personally, was a capacity to fall asleep in a moving vehicle whatever the circumstances. It was especially helpful when hitching overnight, although usually I felt that in some way I had a moral duty to engage the driver in conversation. One thing I acquired from this was a capacity to tune in to the interests and idiom of a wide range of travelling people. For instance in most lorry cabs it was obligatory to get in the F-word at regular intervals to achieve the correct ratio of swear words to sentence typical of the trucker's argot. After a few years I was also pretty clued up on the inadequacies of Foden's lorries, the superiority of the Scania, their speed capabilities under load and the complexities of the tachograph.

I learnt one blustery September night somewhere in the middle of Somerset that it was never a good idea to confront the driver with any opposing point of view. On this particular occasion I was on my way overnight to the Scilly Isles from Norwich, a mere 390 miles. The young guy driving was a soldier just returned from the Falklands conflict. Like all undergraduates during the Thatcher years I was an apostle of world peace and nuclear disarmament. It became a rather ugly exchange when I questioned Britain's right to Las Malvinas. I got my desserts. He dropped me at midnight on a roundabout with traffic that averaged about one car an hour. I had to walk miles into town and catch the Penzance train at two in the morning. (I now realise, of course, the man was a hero. How could we conceive of leaving those seabird colonies to the mercies of the Argentinians?)

I eventually acquired the art of suspended judgement. In a sense this bore a relationship to birding itself: a verbal version of seeing but not being seen. No matter how opposed I might be to the position of my driver, I kept silent. In truth it was worse because I used to like to egg them on to see how extreme they might be. A memorable example was a business rep, a former barrow-boy from the Manchester markets and classic exponent of working-class machismo, but he was taking

63

me to Worksop from Norwich and who was I to jeopardise a valuable lift? He soon gave me the low-down on the collapse of his first relationship. I could appreciate why they'd parted when he said, 'Just after we married I said to Edith, I'm goowin' down pub wi' me mates. And if me Sunday dinner i'n't on table when I get back, thee's trouble.'

Somehow he'd now found a new girlfriend living in north Norfolk. When they'd first made love he claimed to be in danger of a heart attack. '*Euhhh*', he said, a mixture of northern sneer and sexual frisson, 'she's the kinda bird that when she comes inta pub, you put down yer pint-pot and watch every move she maykes!' I could hardly contain myself. In fact at one point he turned to me while driving and fixed me with a fierce glare: 'Are yoo tekkin' piss' or wot?'

Hitching stories were important currency amongst young birders. A record time, a flash car like a Jag or Merc, a near-miss, a mad driver, a kind driver who went miles out of his way – all were grist to the mill in the birders' cycle of tales. It was often a case of the worse the experience, the better the tale. Long waits always had an epic quality and I dimly recall one classic, without being able to link it definitely to a name, of a nine-hour wait at a Glasgow service station. My own personal worst was four days to reach the south of France. After day one I'd got as far as Calais. I'd set out from London that morning and by the French port my average was about seven miles an hour. A third of that had been completed by ferry. At that pace it would have taken eight weeks to reach the Côte d'Azur.

Another occupational hazard was the gay pick-up. Most birders faced it at one time or another. In fact many had been offered a lift by the same chap, who lived in southern Cornwall. He claimed to be an artist and his usual line was to ask if you'd come back to his studio to pose. In the more homophobic ethos of the 1970s he was known as the Poofter of Penzance. Birders used to compare notes on these different personal encounters. I doubt the fellow ever got his drawings of a young male – naked, presumably, except for the pair of bins round the neck – but his persistence meant he provided a valuable service to ornithology, ferrying destitute birders to and from the Scilly Isles.

At worst this kind of lift ended in premature eviction from the car, perhaps if the birder got nervous, or the driver's spurned advances wounded his *amour propre*. But there was one apocryphal legend about a gay lift who requested a birder oblige him with a length of rubber . . . Of course, we never believed it.

A story that was indubitably true belongs to Alan Eardley. In fact Alan's is probably the all-time hitching horror story. He was on his way to Woodfield Spa, Lincolnshire for a Roller. Rollers are beautiful creatures about the size of a Eurasian Jay. With bright fox-red mantles and bluish heads, they are typical birds of southern European grassland. However, when they take flight, unfurling a pair of brilliant azure and royal blue wings, this Mediterranean classic looks more like a fragment of the tropics. To see one in Britain, where there have been just 230 ever, is very special.

When Alan set out to see the Woodfield Spa Roller his father's lift to the A50 near Stoke-on-Trent got the journey off to a routine start. Nor was there anything exceptional about the next lift to Derby, although the third, on a motorbike, was a novel way to get to Radford near Nottingham. Thereafter Alan's memory of the events of 7 October 1983 begins to falter. He recalls it starting to rain when an articulated lorry stopped to pick him up. He also remembers that the driver suggested he put his soaked cagoule by the cab heater. Half an hour later, close to Lincoln, by RAF Swinderby, the picture is blank. His account was pieced together afterwards from friends, relatives and the staff of the emergency services.

Apparently a car ahead of them stopped suddenly, causing Alan's lorry driver to slam on the brakes. In the greasy conditions the vehicle jack-knifed into the path of another oncoming lorry. The massive force of the collision sliced Alan's cab completely off its chassis and sent him clear through its windscreen, through the windscreen of the oncoming vehicle and out through its back window. He was found on the roadside amidst a carpet of shattered glass, thirty metres from the point of impact.

There were almost no visible wounds, but he was unconscious for four days in Lincoln on a life-support machine and remained in hospital in Stoke for the next eight weeks. When he left he was still unable to walk. Immediately after he came round some friends went to visit Alan and tried to stimulate his attention by showing him pictures in bird books. It was clearly serious. He couldn't identify one of them. During the period of coma itself, with his parents at his bedside, Alan was classified 'critically ill' with a 60 per cent chance of mortality. 'The Roller', he concluded, 'was probably one of the biggest mega-dips that's happened.'

The most mere mortals could usually hope to share round the campfire of an evening was the story of a really long hitch in a single lift. The ultimate, the hitching equivalent of the jackpot, achieved by a handful on their way from Fair Isle in Shetland to the Scillies – and probably representing the longest feasible hitch in the British Isles – was a single lift on the 683-mile drive from Aberdeen to Penzance. My own best for distance was a paltry 300-mile Knutsford-to-Perth run in a minibus. And for style my top hitch was a TV director (unknown) for the first leg, then a Porsche from Norwich to London.

But it didn't matter that I never claimed any hitching records. Right to the end the whole business of hitching retained a certain element of adventure. 'Where are you going, mate?' the first words uttered prior to any lift, were an open sesame to a peculiar kind of satisfaction. In the film *The Colour of Money*, Paul Newman's character, Fast Eddy, declares that money won is twice as sweet as money earned. Hitching bears a similar relationship to any other form of transport. And in a way its gratifications are a corollary to those of birding itself. There was always a degree of uncertainty. You were at the mercy of pure chance and it was precisely that risk of failure which gave the edge to its undeniable pleasures. Yet nothing made you feel more in control of your destiny than to get to the target location, to thank that last lift for the final leg of your journey, and swing a rucksack up on to your back. Just momentarily you savoured the absolute autonomy of the tribal nomad.

I give you one last example of a classic hitch which embodies all the specific joys and agonies that belonged to the birder on the road. It involved Clive Byers and Dick Filby. Clive is now an internationally recognised bird illustrator with a large body of work published in numerous books, most notably in the multi-volume *Handbook of the Birds of the World*. Dick travels the world leading wildlife holidays and has visited Antarctica twenty-one times. He also runs Bird Alert, the original birders' paging service and major competitor to Paul Flint's company. Both Clive and Dick are successful professionals in the world of birds.

But in July 1973 they were teenage schoolboys and keen twitchers. During the holidays both decided to hitch for the Steller's Eider at Vorran Island on South Uist. Nowadays, with a paging service like the one Dick runs, birders can keep almost minute-by-minute tabs on rare birds. But in the 1970s bird information, which was always referred to as 'the gen', was often old. In the case of the Steller's Eider the gen was several months old. No one had seen it since the spring.

But on that July morning Dick and Clive are completely undeterred. They take the tube to Hendon Central to walk to the bottom of the A1/M1. The plan is an extended tour of Scotland, including the trip to South Uist, prefaced by a stop at Clumber Park in Nottinghamshire for an uncommon raptor called a Honey Buzzard. The whole trip is around 2000 miles. Unfortunately none of the drivers during that first hour of hitching are aware of this timetable. Worse, half the teenage and student population of north London seems to have similar ideas of a holiday up north. At eight in the morning the line of hitchers already stretches for hundreds of yards and those at the front have theoretical priority.

I say *theoretical* because the people actually giving lifts are not bound by the hitchers' code of conduct. They have no sense of duty to the man who's been there longest. They stop for whomever they like the look of. Clive and Dick are two young males, one of them well over six foot, with huge rucksacks holding supplies for a fortnight, complete with tent and dangling boots. Two hours later they're still at the back of the queue.

Three hours later and the plans are beginning to shift. The idea of stopping at Clumber is jettisoned in favour of a straight run all the way through to Scotland. Unfortunately none of the drivers gets this changed schedule either. Four hours later and they're still there.

I theorise here on how Clive and Dick felt. But had *I* been there for four hours it's at this point in a hitch I'd begin to calculate how the morning's eight o'clock train to Edinburgh would have already reached its destination. Then you try to put temptation at the back of your mind and take the initiative. For instance you try to ensure friendly eye-contact with every single passing driver just in case you can ignite that flickering sense of social conscience. Unfortunately after five hours you're so pissed off with the waiting and keeping up the false smile, your friendly eye-contact looks more like the evil eye.

After six hours you hate all the smug bastards steaming past in their precious cars. You vow, there and then, that when you get a car you'll never ever pass a hitcher on the roadside in the rest of your life. You also vow you're *never* going to hitch again. You're hungry. You're paralysed with boredom. You wish you'd never had the idea in the first place. You're just about to pick up your rucksack and . . . Then a car stops.

Dick and Clive shout, 'We're going up north.' 'Yeah, jump in.'

Truth to tell, having stood there until two in the afternoon,

Clive and Dick probably couldn't care where he's heading. Anywhere but that stretch of kerb. They simply climb aboard. Or, at least, they try to climb aboard. But this is a Mini. The driver already has two huge suitcases on the back seat. Clive wedges himself next to these and seals himself in with the huge rucksack on his lap. Dick, who's over six foot, shoehorns himself into the front seat with his own rucksack on his knees. And off they go. About twenty minutes down the road they realise they ought to pop the hitcher's standard question.

Back comes the answer. Inverness!

Dick and Clive relax into their seats and the cares of the morning fall away. It slowly begins to dawns on them. The world can be a truly beautiful place.

Through the afternoon and long summer evening they drive steadily north and into the Scottish highlands, where their chauffeur goes out of his way to drop them at the turning for Fort William. They hitch into town, pitch their tent and in the morning wake to a rolling bank of Atlantic cloud. It begins to rain torrentially. By early afternoon they make it into Mallaig, where unfortunately there's no ferry until the day after next. And still it rains. Boredom threatens. In desperation and in rain, for the first and only time in their lives, they go fishing and catch a mullet.

Eventually the ferry comes, the rain stops and they board. Several hours later they sight the low dark evening contours of Barra, the southernmost of the archipelago. Then on the ferry ploughs towards its larger neighbour, the island of South Uist. Way off to the east Dick and Clive can see the jagged outline of Skye crowned by the blackened peaks of the Cuillin Hills. To the west are the white shell-sand beaches that are the trademark of the low-lying Uists. Eighty-six hours ago the two of them were walking out of Hendon Central, now they descend the gangplank a world away on the Outer Hebrides. Even at midnight it's still light and more in hope than expectation they throw out a thumb and catch their second fish – and the second Mini – of the trip.

It's actually the local vicar who's stopped. He seems not to have any particular destination himself and out of Christian charity he drives Clive and Dick out of the port at Lochboisdale, up to the main north–south road on the island, on past the first in an endless sequence of tiny pools and lochans, which make South Uist as much a waterscape as a land form; on past the tiny crofters' hamlets with their unpronounceable Gaelic names; down a tiny side lane, then he steers at right angles on to a simple farm track and soon even this basic thoroughfare is left behind them as they plough out across an open field to the point on the coast immediately opposite Vorran Island. The day before yesterday Clive and Dick had intimations. Now they know: the world is a truly, truly beautiful place.

In the morning they wake to a chorus of Skylarks and Corncrakes and through the intoxicating, champagne-clear air of the Outer Hebrides they can make out the exquisite form of a male *Polysticta stelleri* just offshore; only the eighth ever to be recorded. In seeing that Steller's Eider, they witness a fragment of British ornithological history and in travelling for four days and 700 miles Clive and Dick have, in a sense, become a part of that history themselves.

There are four lovely postcripts to their hitch to Vorran Island.

1. About a fortnight later. The two of them are both back at the bottom of the M1/A1 near to Hendon Central, hitching for another bird further north. It's the same routine: a great line of hitchers all ahead of them, streams of traffic pouring past, refusing to stop. Then suddenly a carful of four come past, stare at Clive and Dick and screech to a halt. They're all birders. Everyone knows each other. But, no, they can't give them a lift. They're full. Besides, they say – with an ever-so-slightly-detectable note of smugness – *they're* off to the Outer Hebrides for Steller's Eider.

Back, instantly, comes a great snort of derision and much Latin waving of arms. Steller's Eider! Pfffff. Did that YEARS ago!

2. Twenty-six years later. Dick's in Norwich and happens to recount, for some inexplicable reason, his and Clive's epic hitch to the Outer Hebrides to a woman who lives locally. When it comes to the part about the rector and the Mini out across the fields right to Vorran Island itself, the woman's face lights up unexpectedly. The good vicar is her brother-in-law. She phones to tell him about the extraordinary coincidence. He remembers Dick and Clive clearly. You see, the world *is* a beautiful place.

3. Twenty-seven years later, on 4 November 2000 Dick twitches the Outer Hebrides for only the second time in his life. The bird is a Long-tailed Shrike, a first for Britain, and it's just a couple of miles down the road from Vorran Island. Remember, getting to the Steller's Eider took eighty-six hours. For the shrike, Dick sets off at six-thirty in the morning from Norwich, sees the bird, and arrives back in Norwich at three-thirty in the afternoon. The whole journey, 1310 miles, takes nine hours in total in a friend's plane.

4. A few weeks after the epic hitch. Clive is on the East Bank at Cley in Norfolk and as he stands there a young twitcher approaches him with a strong northern accent, a Pancho Villa moustache and a falcon's look of intensity. They're soon in conversation and Clive gets round to the Steller's Eider. He describes its location and the bird's gorgeous appearance: the delicate apricot breast and flanks, the long white scapulars flopped to one side in bold relief against purple-tinged tertials, a soft white head with its crisp black necklace and that curious isolated spot of olive-green on the nape. Within minutes the northern birder is sold. He buys Clive's old battered map of the Outer Hebrides and walks back along East Bank.

Remember. He's just hitched 170 miles down to Norfolk for a few days, birding. But he's decided – there and then – to go to South Uist. Think of it. It's 750 miles just to the Hebrides. There and back to his house it's about 1350 miles. Through the rain, the wind, and a long cold Scottish night, he won't stop until he's seen the bird. I could never have done it then. I certainly couldn't do it today and even now it strikes me as heroic.

Oh yes. The young twitcher's name? Paul Flint.

What Paul did that day, was very much representative of that period. In post-Thatcherite Britain the whole business of hitching seems to have become far too risky for both parties and you hardly ever see anybody at the roadside with a thumb out. You certainly never see anybody with bins strung round his neck. Birders just don't do it any more. That vision belongs to a more innocent era – the 1970s – and it's perhaps partly for this reason that many birders look back on the decade as part of a golden age.

Back then, if you could have got into some hypothetical control module in space where you could monitor birders' movements around Britain's road networks, the screen would have appeared as an endless chaos of random blips, each one representing young twitchers hitching back and forth across the country. There were would have been occasional patterns – clusters heading towards Norfolk in May, a brief lull in July, a further rush towards Shetland in September, or Cornwall in October. There would never have been a single moment when there were no blips registered on the screen.

Nor would all the blips ever be clustered at a single spot. But if you could have watched each trajectory over the decade, almost all would have intersected at one point. That place was the East Bank at Cley. And this much is indubitably true. At one time or another that 750-yard strip of mud track has borne the impress of *every* single keen able-bodied birder in Britain.

On 23 June 1976 Tog and I were heading for that spot. In the meantime, however, we were stuck in the Lincolnshire village of Sutterton and to cover the additional seventy miles to Cley would take us another whole day. At hitching we were hopeless amateurs, but we were in no hurry. Buxton was behind us. The tent was pitched on the back lawn of a pub, The Angel. I was sixteen. Tog was seventeen. Sleeves rolled, we were celebrating the day's varied achievements with a pint and a game of darts. On our taste buds was the raw, satisfying, bitter-sweet blend of lager with lime and cheap cigar smoke. A quarter of a century later I cannot recover the sensations of that evening exactly. But one flavour still rings clear as on the day itself. It was the unmistakable taste of freedom.

9

A Godwit's Inscrutable Eye

Several breeding pairs, Black-tailed Godwit, Limosa limosa
Cley, Norfolk 1968–70

A person's attachment to a particular landscape is always a question of individual taste. But some love affairs need less explanation than others. Is it difficult, for instance, to comprehend a passion for the Orkneys or Shetlands? I don't think so. You cannot visit Hoy or Fair Isle without being awed by the power of the Atlantic and the dizzying scale of the sea cliffs. It's easy to be lulled by the harsh poetry of the crofters' lifestyle, the community's lilting dialect, their love of music and the aesthetic possibilities of spun wool. The islanders' tight-knit intimacy with these northern landscapes and their rugged self-sufficiency render them as distinct from those bustling up the Vauxhall Bridge Road as a nomadic tribe from inner Asia. Even if we don't feel it ourselves, we *understand* the allure of their environment.

Cley isn't like that. North Norfolk doesn't wow you with its sublimity like the Northern Isles, or enfold you in the picturesque like the Scillies. It lacks the romance associated with offshore islands. In fact the Norfolk coast can seem flat, hard, stony, prosaic. Bogged down in mist or sticky and enervated from baking sunshine, you can be either frozen to the bone or burnt like a lobster. Its sheer emptiness leaves you nowhere to hide.

For birders it has such a reputation that they have go there, but on first sight many find the place a huge anti-climax. I did. By the time of my first visit I'd been sold the *idea* of Cley for the previous three years. Tog had been there in August 1973 and he never let me forget. I'd nursed a deep envy of him ever since, although I got my revenge. I moved to Norfolk two years after that first visit and have lived there ever since. Tog, because of job or circumstances, has lived elsewhere. We often discuss his moving to Norfolk as if it were actually a return to his rightful place, like the homecoming of an exile.

But in truth I am not as content as I might seem. I live in Norwich, not Cley. I've lived in Saxthorpe, ten miles inland, and at Holkham and Brancaster, both a few miles along the coast, but never in Cley itself. I am also, in a sense, in internal exile, barred from that place in my heart which the village has occupied since the late 1970s.

One of the difficulties of living there is the sheer cost of houses. Strung out for about a mile, they wander the line of an old medieval harbour on the banks of a vanished estuary which once stretched inland for two miles up the River Glaven. The tidal waters which washed up to the village doorstep on its western fringe have long since been shut out by land-reclamation banks built in the nineteenth century and Cley port itself has gone completely. Most of the village stands at least a mile from open seawater. But the air of maritime trade lingers still. Its church, St Margaret's, is a grand, weathered sandstone monument to a bustling medieval past, while two of the larger houses on the main road are the old customs house and the town hall. A town hall in a village of about 500 souls speaks volumes about Cley's former prosperity. Many of the other houses are also large, old and full of character, and Cley has become a classic retirement locality, which has pushed house prices well beyond the norm elsewhere in the county.

Not that these economic issues bothered Tog and I as we walked through the village after our two-day hitch from Buxton. We'd everything we needed: two pubs, the George and the Three Swallows, a low-priced café known as Nancy's and a shop called the Whalebone Stores specialising in bird books and Alwych notebooks. What more – I asked myself – could a village possibly offer?

But our main concern was the birds. Or rather the apparent lack of them. Cley was legendary for rarities, especially rare waders. The full list for the place runs to about fifty of these long-legged, long-billed species. We or, at least, *I* was expecting freshwater pools smothered in busy flocks. But there were no pools and those we could see were on the reserve itself, behind fences that bore perimeter signs announcing entry for permit-holders only. The reserve is owned and managed by the Norfolk Wildlife Trust (known until 1994 as the Norfolk Naturalists Trust or the NNT) and at that time even its members had to pay for access. To teenage non-members it was prohibitively expensive – about our daily budget for food. It looked as if we'd hitched for two days to see Cley but not its legendary birds.

In time, like most other young birders, we learned to go without permits and acquired the knack of judicious trespass, watching out for the unmistakable stocky figure of Cley's legendary warden, Billy Bishop. If the coast was clear we'd sneak out to the hides to see whatever unusual birds were on show at that moment. Of course I wouldn't do it now. (At least, not now that Trust membership gives you free access.) And if there are any youngsters reading this: DON'T DO IT! It's illegal, it stunts your growth and Bernard (Billy's son and heir as Cley warden) will give you a good bollocking if he catches you.

Fortunately we quickly learnt two other important aspects of birding at Cley. Outstanding bird spot though it is, Cley is merely the central gemstone in a great necklace of wonderful birding locations that runs virtually the length of the north coast, from Sheringham in the east to Hunstanton in the west. In truth it is the *whole* coast that makes Norfolk such a special place for birders. (It's this fact that softens my exile from Cley, since Norwich is strategically placed for access to the whole thirty-mile stretch.) So in June 1976 the fact we couldn't get on to Cley reserve wasn't so serious. There were other wonderful sites beckoning like Salthouse Heath, Blakeney Point, Holkham and Titchwell.

The other critical piece of information we soon acquired was that even at Cley itself visiting the actual reserve was something most birders did only rarely. Although the reedbeds and pools owned by the Trust were off-limits, the shingle beach and the defensive sea walls on the east and west perimeters, which enclose this tide-threatened marsh on three sides, were not. And the centre of all birding activity was the raised embankment that marked the reserve's boundary furthest from the village, East Bank.

Roughly half a mile long, East Bank occupies an interesting position on a map of the British Isles, in fact, of the whole northern hemisphere. It runs due north and lies about one degree, four minutes east of the Greenwich meridian. At the far end of the bank you arrive at the beach. Beyond is the North Sea and if you were to maintain the same course across the water you wouldn't strike *terra firma* until you'd crossed the North Pole and the Arctic pack ice and arrived on the other side of the world about 4000 miles away at Wrangel Island off the north-east coast of Siberia. In 1976 it definitely had a strong sense of place. Although we headed towards it that June afternoon, not to savour any terminal atmosphere, but in order to meet the person whose own legend was integral to that of Cley itself, the late Richard Richardson.

It's at this point in the story that I feel I need to get up from my desk, walk over to where you're now sitting and then take a pen and poke a hole in the fabric of the narrative. If you now put your eye to that opening you'll see me seated back at my computer and on the desk is a plan of the book. Run your eye quickly down the column of chapter headings and you'll see, inserted between titles eight and nine, a hand-drawn arrow pointing towards three letters in small block capitals, 'RAR'.

I have to confess that an account of Richard Alan Richardson wasn't scheduled in my original synopsis. If you like, he was an afterthought. But as I went to talk to all the birders who feature in this book I was overwhelmed by the outpouring of deep and genuine affection for the man. In describing the development of their own birding, most of my interviewees said something along the lines of, 'And then I went to Cley and, of course, met Richard Richardson . . .' My sample may be biased, since I mainly spoke to birders who live in or near East Anglia, but if this was an accurate straw poll then Richard is one of the most popular, the most revered, the most remembered birders from the second half of the twentieth century, possibly from the whole century.

By itself this certainly renders his life story of interest to birders. But at the heart of his reputation I found a curious puzzle and its explanation gives to Richard's tale a far deeper resonance; one that offers insights into birding culture and also the very nature of what it means to be a human being hooked on birds.

And here is that central mystery. Richard Richardson was a famous birder and bird artist. I'd heard of him years before I met him – a recurring and central *dramatis persona* in the cycle of tribal stories – but if you examine his record you'll not find a formal body of achievement and work that by itself seems to justify the high esteem with which his name is surrounded. So *why* exactly is Richard so highly regarded?

Let's start at the beginning. He was born in 1922, a sailor's illegitimate son, in a working-class district of Blackheath in south London. He was apparently brought up as an orphan in a children's home and it's tempting at this stage to invent an early passion for inarticulate nature as a foil for the kind of emotional turmoil which seems implicit in his childhood circumstances. But truth to tell, not much is known about his early life except that in later years he kept in regular touch with his Aunt Ethel in Bournemouth, and that his first link with his adopted home came during the Second World War, when he served in the Royal Norfolk Regiment.

Apparently he did a stint in India and south-east Asia and spent a year in Singapore following the Japanese surrender in 1945. There's no doubt that he was already keen on birds and became familiar with Oriental species which, while common in Asia, appear from time to time on Britain's east coast as wind-blown vagrants. The war had given Richard a head start in the business of finding rarities on the Norfolk coast.

That was where the young twenty-seven-year-old headed on his return to Britain, apparently first introduced to the place by a wealthy older woman who was impressed by his drawings. In 1949 he settled as a lodger in a Cley house rented by an elderly widow, Mrs Davison, and eventually became like her adopted son, moving with her when she herself swapped houses within the village. She was a tough, feisty Norfolk woman, one of those odd characters who always seem to have been old. To most of Richard's young friends, who christened her 'Grunge', she seemed ancient and witch-like when he moved in. Twenty-seven years later when Richard was being buried in Cley churchyard, she seemed ancient still. But Grunge outlived him by several years and died in her nineties.

Richard's own migration to Norfolk was itself a response to the county's existing reputation as the foremost bird spot in mainland Britain, and Cley reserve was at the heart of that status. It had been established in 1926, one of the first nature reserves ever to be created in Britain, but this pioneering purchase had, in turn, been a recognition of the area's pre-existing renown for birds. So Richard's residence in the village was part of a tradition stretching back into the nineteenth century. And it's a tradition that continues to this day. Cley and the surrounding villages probably have a higher proportion of birders per head of population than anywhere else on the planet.

Although Cley was renowned as a place to see birds, there was no formal establishment to take advantage of its ornithological importance. So in 1949 Richard set up the Cley Bird Observatory, with initial sponsorship from the Norfolk Naturalists Trust. In the postwar years there were observatories at a number of key birding locations. St Agnes in the Scillies had one, for example, and Fair Isle still does. Until the 1960s they were probably the principal focus for birding activity, and they were usually a cheap hostel-style accommodation where amateur ornithologists can go to share in the advancement of scientific knowledge. As an institution the observatory had its origins in the communal ethos of an older Britain, and nowadays that collective spirit towards the pastime seems both old-fashioned and quaint.

While they reflected a purposeful approach to birds, I learnt at Spurn Head that observatories were also wonderfully informal, rather ramshackle establishments, ideal for a cheap holiday surrounded by like-minded people, where you could talk, read, breathe, sleep, dream and hatch wild schemes about birds for weeks at a stretch. That recreational spirit runs counter to the large amount of organisation needed to keep these shoestring operations running smoothly. And it would perhaps be true to say that organisation wasn't Richard's forte.

Nor was he very lucky in his management of Cley Bird Observatory. The building itself, the headquarters and general storeroom, was close to the beach and a stone's throw away from the sea, the same sea that continues uninterrupted to Wrangel Island. As well as stretching 4000 miles one way, it has an irritating habit of extending its range in the other direction, storming up the beach and through the embankments at Cley. The great surge tide in January 1953 buried the environs of the observatory in five feet of shingle, while the Heligoland traps, large funnel-shaped structures used for catching birds for ringing purposes, were engulfed in a massive slick of pebbles nine feet thick. Although Richard and his helpers rebuilt some of the traps and constructed new ones elsewhere, these were also demolished by winter gales several years later.

In the period that it existed a grand total of 17,544 birds were

ringed at Cley, no small achievement in itself. But Britain's ninth
bird observatory was destined to be one of the shortest lived.
Fourteen years after it opened, its honorary warden duly retired
at the ripe old age of forty-one. It was a good innings, but it
didn't really represent a lasting memorial to the man. Nor did
it reflect Richard's most natural talent.

Most people saw this as his gift for painting and drawing
birds. He was a self-taught artist who'd already illustrated two
books before the observatory closed, entitled *The pocket guide
to British birds* and *The pocket guide to nests and eggs*, published by
Collins in 1952 and 1955 respectively. Both were collaborations
with the naturalist and author, Richard Fitter.

In its day, the first of Richardson's two titles was groundbreaking,
which said much about its main competitors like *The Observer's
Book of Birds*. Even at the genesis of my own birding *The
Observer's* was still going strong and about the only book I
could readily lay my hands on in Buxton. At five and a
half inches tall, the book was perfect for the pocket. The
trouble was only half the plates were in colour. The rest
were monochrome. It meant you could only identify every
other bird. If you happened to be looking at a species depicted
in black and white, you had to guess the colours represented
by various tones of grey. It was a nightmare.

Worse, however, was the fact that they weren't really
illustrations designed specifically to aid the novice. They were
paintings, little fragments of art, fulfilling their creator, Archibald
Thorburn's, notions of romance, of pathos, of the picturesque
and the sublime as expressed through the lives of birds. They
were truly lovely but they were *ancient*. He'd painted them
originally in the 1890s for Lord Lilford's book, *Coloured Figures
of the Birds of the British Isles*. Identifying birds with these was like
someone trying to build a modern family car using the original
design plans drawn up by Charles Rolls and Henry Royce.

Richard moved the whole business of a bird-identification
guide on into the modern era. Instead of listing birds in
taxonomic sequence, reflecting their presumed evolutionary

relationships, Fitter and Richardson chose to put species with similar appearances on the same page, in order to highlight the main points of difference. Most books gave you one illustration per bird, possibly two if sexes differ. But this is hopeless when species, like the gannet and all the gulls, evolve through a sequence of different plumages as they mature from juvenile to adult. To deal with this kind of complexity Richard depicted the birds at their different stages.

He also offered criteria for identifying birds which had never been considered as readily separable before. For instance, most books only dealt with the separation of one species from another. But by depicting birds like White and Pied Wagtail, both then considered races of the same species, Richard took identification a stage further. He even showed them in their summer *and* their winter plumages. It was the kind of nuance that in many ways reflected the man and Richard was above all a sophisticated field observer.

Trouble was, so too were Guy Mountfort and Phil Hollom and their American friend, the artist Roger Tory Peterson (he of Oystercatcher fame at Hilbre Island). Just two years after Richard's plates appeared, the three of them produced the closest thing to a revolution in bird books, a work called *A Field Guide to the Birds of Britain and Europe*. Richardson's plates were good, but Peterson's were better.

The bold, accurate colours and diagrammatic formula of the American artist's birds completely eclipsed the Englishman's achievement. They captured exactly what the beginner birder needs to achieve an identification. 'Peterson', as it came to be known, was an instant bestseller and, remarkably, nearly fifty years later is still adding to its million-plus sales in thirteen foreign-language editions. Today it's finally starting to lose ground to the latest generation of bird field guides. But if Peterson now looks tired, Richard's books have the air of historical documents, reflections of a vanished past.

Some of his work survived longer. For example, his lovely vignettes, casual black-and-white sketches that he might have knocked off in a spare hour, continued to appear in the annual publication known as the *Norfolk Bird and Mammal Report* right until the end of the 1990s, twenty years after Richard himself had died. But I've always interpreted this inclusion of Richard's work, not so much as a measure of his ongoing parity with the latest bird illustrators but, latterly, as a way for the publication's editor, Michael Seago, to continue to honour the great man's legend. They were tributes to the memory of an old friend in a publication Richard had himself helped to establish. And why not? But like the Cley Bird Observatory, Richard's artwork doesn't quite justify the renown.

I turn now to the slenderest portion of RAR's work – his writing. I should preface this by saying that no case can be made for Richard as a serious player in ornithological literature quite simply because he hardly ever published anything. He was a routine contributor to the *Norfolk Bird and Mammal Report*, often writing a brief account of migration at Cley, but the rest of his pieces were infrequent and short. There was a note on a hirundine *ménage à trois* entitled 'Bigamy in Swallow'. There was a little paper on the very first occurrence of the Collared Dove, that beige-coloured pigeon that's now conquered the British Isles from end to end (and whose song a friend describes as like a bored football fan – 'U-ni-téd! – U-ni-téd! – U-ni-téd! – U-ni-téd!).

There was also a brief, co-authored essay on a Radde's Warbler, the first ever seen in Norfolk and only the second record for Britain. It was one of those Far Eastern species which Richard might just possibly have seen during his war years in Asia and there's a wonderful little footnote that I can't resist. When they first trapped it they couldn't quite be sure it was a Radde's, so they put it in Richard's outdoor aviary for the night while Ken Williamson, Britain's leading authority on *Phylloscopus* warblers, rushed down from Scotland to check it out.

Richard's most important piece of bird literature, apart from his books, was an account of breeding behaviour of

the Black-tailed Godwit. The bird is one of the largest and
most beautiful of those fifty wader species recorded at Cley. It
once occurred widely across the wetlands of East Anglia, but
by the early nineteenth century had been evicted as a breeding
species as a consequence of hunting and drainage schemes. For
the next hundred years there were only a scattering of records,
so when a handful of birds started to show signs of nesting at
Cley in the mid-1960s there was much excitement. Richard
was at the forefront of the efforts to protect and monitor the
rarity's return and his account of their fortunes was published
in three successive issues of the *Norfolk Bird and Mammal Report*
from 1968 to 1970.

It was ornithological writing far removed from the sawdust
and straitjacket of modern scientific literature. Take this passage
on the effects of torrential rain on a brooding bird: 'Male C
relieved his mate at noon and sat as if petrified throughout
the afternoon, becoming progressively wetter as the minutes
dragged by. Huddled in the nest, with white eyelids tightly
shut and swallowing the raindrops as they trickled down his
bill, he was the epitomy [sic] of dejection.'

Here's his description of a displaying male: 'The wings moved
alternately . . . one half flexed, the other fully spread . . . and the
fanned tail swerved first to one side and then to the other, the
body rocking drunkenly as the bird limped about the sky.'

But the passage I love most occurs in the second of his
trilogy. Note, especially, the forensically detailed observations
and the author's openly emotional disclosures:

The second week of May was comparatively uneventful
in the godwit world. Pair C had obviously accepted the
proximity of the Hide and its inhabitants and, provided
one kept out of sight, it was possible to carry on a
normal conversation without upsetting them. It was a
delight just to sit with one's eye to the telescope and
enjoy the enchanting picture, filling the field of view,
of a godwit on its nest. Many were the occasions when

I tried to penetrate beyond that inscrutable eye in which the reflection of the Hide could clearly be seen. That the sitting bird was happy I had no doubt, watching the comings and goings or drowsing contentedly in the rare gleams of sunshine. A fly basked on the black and copper plumage until the feathers were ruffled by a sudden breeze or the bird reached forward to retrieve an errant blade of grass, half rising to tuck it carefully into the nest . . .

It is as beautiful an image of a nesting bird as Richard ever created with paintbrush and watercolours, and I reproduce it here because it shows that he was a far better writer than his output suggested; also because it tells me much about why his star still burns so brightly.

Some people thought that Richard hadn't just attempted 'to penetrate beyond that inscrutable eye' – and let's face it, the ambition alone is remarkable – but that he'd actually managed to achieve it. It's this identification with birds which helps explain an aspect of Richard on which all his friends and acquaintances are unanimous. He was a brilliant birder.

The environmental writer, Richard Mabey, his friend during the 1960s and 1970s, described Richard's 'uncanny knack of being able to see the world from a bird's point of view'.

He could turn migrating golden plovers and whimbrels round in the sky by whistling their contact calls, and predict from which invisible spot ground-nesting birds would fly up. I remember his gazing at a flock of terns wafting in to fish in the pools and saying, 'It would be worth a skua's while . . .'. It was. A minute or so later an Arctic skua . . . slid in over the sea wall and began harrying the terns.

Another of Richardson's gifts was exceptional eyesight. His close friend, Ron Johns, suggested he had the best eyesight of any birder he's ever known and other stories confirm that verdict. Richard could see and identify birds at a huge range, before his companions had even spotted them. And to those of us, like me, who don't possess, or have lost this kind of visual acuity, it is an almost magical talent, compelling both admiration and envy.

A comparable sort of cult probably exists in the world of shooting. I'm sure a brilliant left and right can earn you an enduring reputation. But in birding you only get one fluke. The rest have to be based on something else, both rare and special, and Richardson's genius, according to Richard Mabey, was 'an astonishing ability to recognize birds by their "jizz"'.

Jizz is an arcane but much-bandied term in birding parlance. Originally it was probably a piece of military jargon, but it now refers to each separate bird's indefinable, almost inarticulable visual 'personality'. It's what Gerard Manley Hopkins might have described as the bird's *inscape*. In Buddhist metaphysics it would probably be termed the bird's *isness*: an inward fabric of characteristics which crystallise out in some unique and recognisable identity. Personally, being a far more limited, outside-looking-in sort of birder I find it difficult to grasp and feel much more comfortable with the notion that all the bird's individual qualities are accountable in terms of observable quantities. But other birders are much more at home with this subjective *feel* for the bird. To them jizz has been elevated to a kind of spiritual art, the Zen of birding.

And if it had a spiritual master, Richard was it. His artwork, almost inevitably, is very jizzy, both in the sense that as soon as you see a Richardson you can recognise its author instantly; but also in the sense that 'his' birds are themselves recognisably doing things and behaving as they would in real life. They had a definite quality of living authenticity.

But an extraordinary thing about Richard's art was that he never sketched in the field. Most of his work was done from memory at the kitchen table in Mrs Davison's house. Was it laziness? Possibly. I also think it was a gift for going beyond 'the inscrutable eye' that enabled him to reproduce the beast unaided on the blank page. Don't get me wrong. I wouldn't wish to make great claims for his art. It can look inaccurate in terms of the bird's shape and proportions. But compare his work with two other, undeniably greater bird artists. There was no drawing from freshly dead skins, hauled into exaggerated, often contorted, postures on a framework of wires, as Audubon did. (In fact stuffed skins are still the basic reference for almost all modern illustrators.) Nor were birds reduced to a diagrammatic two-dimensional formula, as in Peterson's ground-breaking set of plates. The birds were as they are.

I speculate whether it was this existential journey into the life of his fellow creatures that explains other aspects of his personality, such as his apparent lack of concern to achieve the 'ordinary' goals of human life. Richard never married. He never owned a house. He didn't seem too concerned about either accumulating wealth or attaining worldly success. In the opinion of those who knew him well Richard Richardson seemed a deeply contented man.

His days were simple, geographically circumscribed in a way that few birders would tolerate nowadays, and regulated by a number of fixed rituals. He was, for instance, an inveterate smoker, never without the evil weed that eventually killed him, either in the form of Woodbines or what Richard Mabey described as 'minutely thin roll-ups'. In fact the only words I distinctly remember him saying to me, in a wonderful south London accent, were 'Wanna faaaag?'

An equally unshakable habit was the teenager's mixture of Wrangler denim, Doc Martens and black leather jacket, worn right up until his death at fifty-five. A black French beret was a further exotic touch, but the archetypal rebel image was sealed by his passion for large motorbikes, firstly the Matchless 350, then the Norton Dominator, which he used to cover the single mile's distance from Mrs Davison's to the East Bank. The only breaks to the Norfolk routine were themselves two other set rituals, a twice-yearly visit to Aunt Ethel's in Bournemouth (taking in the New Forest in spring and Portland Bill in the autumn) and a biennial trip to his other great love, Fair Isle. In total he went twenty-three times. Richard's visits to the bird observatory became known as 'Norfolk week' and there he developed secondary attachments to Shetland fiddle music and rare antiquarian books about the archipelago.

But East Bank was undoubtedly his spiritual home. It was a daily pilgrimage, a kind of bird-oriented constitutional, that he never missed. It was where I met him. It was where everyone met him. In fact whenever I even *think* of him, he's there on East Bank. Each time he'd leave the enormous Norton bike in the small car park at the southern end, then walk down almost to the point where East Bank becomes a great ramp of pebbles rising up to the shingle beach.

At about this spot Richard would sit down overlooking Arnold's Marsh, a large salt-water pool to the east of the reserve. The vegetation in that area was flattened and worn over a wide section of one side of the bank (curiously it still is, although no one ever seems to sit there now) because Richard's routine was in fact everyone's routine. That spot was *the* spot. Going to Cley meant sitting or lying down on that same small section of East Bank. Richard Mabey described the unscheduled gatherings around him as 'like ornithological *salons*'.

One of the participants in the impromptu seminars was a boy called Martin Woodcock. Martin is now an internationally recognised bird artist and illustrator, whose 250 plates in the monumental seven-volume *The Birds of Africa* make him one of only a select handful of bird painters ever to have illustrated the avifauna of an entire zoogeographical region. As a teenager on East Bank he too sat and learned at the master's feet. But in this instance the phrase is more than figurative. Only a lucky few could sit next to Richard. The rest had to perch somewhere lower down East Bank around those legendary DMs. Not that this should suggest any element of conceit on Richard's part. No one, so far, has ever suggested the man we all hero-worshipped viewed himself in that light. On the contrary. Richard was a modest man, gentle and encouraging, a stutterer given to self-mockery about his disability.

More than any formal body of work, more than any one of his single achievements – as creator of Cley Bird Observatory, student of migration, illustrator, artist or author – these unscheduled meetings take us right to the heart of Richard's reputation. Nothing was ever written down at these gatherings. Little was ever recorded, apart from the odd photograph, or the occasional drawing on the back of a fag packet, as he illustrated some point of identification. But Richard passed on his massive experience and his love of birds to *everyone* who was willing to listen. It didn't matter who you were. A little old lady on East Bank for the first and only time in her life, or a fellow luminary of the birding establishment, Richard adapted and talked to anyone. The only thing he required was that you show some fraction of his own deep commitment to birds.

It's the blend of all these unrecorded Richard Richardsons I most admire and which is so illuminating of birding mores. There was, on the one hand, the bastard son of a seaman talking on equal terms with the upper-middle-class county establishment, from which constituency the Norfolk Naturalists Trust drew its council and officials. There was the working-class Londoner discussing the finer points of godwit behaviour with a university don or the master of a public school. But there was also Richard Richardson, the famous artist, brilliant fieldman and elder statesman of British birding, patiently encouraging some teenage enthusiast to keep going with his sketches or to consider some new drawing technique to improve their quality.

It was his ability to enthuse and support young people which is commemorated in the two institutional memorials to Richard's name. He himself set up a fund that's still operating, to help cover the costs for a young birder to visit Fair Isle. The Richard Richardson art award was established after his death in 1977 and is given by the journal

British Birds to celebrate the achievements of a new talent in bird art.

But the East Bank ornithological salons and the pool of youngsters who benefited from them are by far the largest of his legacies. It included many of the key players in the modern world of birds: wardens, artists, editors, professional conservationists, authors, publishers, identification experts, brilliant fieldmen. Richard's salons were a proving house for the bird world's future establishment, yet the crucial point is that they were nobody when Richard knew them. What he passed on to that subsequent generation above everything else was that most precious of commodities – himself. He had time for us before we were worth talking to. Now that's a talent really worth remembering.

However, I have to admit it creates a particular kind of reputation. Richard was most famous simply for being himself and he'll remain a revered figure as long as those cherished recollections continue as part of a living imagination. But a figure from folk memory, no matter how influential, is destined to fade.★ In a hundred years time there'll be very little to remind us of who Richard Richardson was, why he was so loved and how he made such an impact. Should we mind? I don't think so.

I don't think he'd have minded. Richard was a man of simple pleasures. But he took a radical decision long before it was socially acceptable: that birds were what mattered in life and he would spend *his* life birding. Very few if any had ever done that before. Those who had were either wealthy enough for it not to matter or academics who fitted in their birding around professional duties. But amongst those from Richard's social background he was the first. Now that lifestyle is part of the pattern of tribal behaviour. Lots of birders take that path. I took it . . . sort of. But when Richard made the choice it required

★ It now looks as if those memories of Richard won't fade, because a biography is just now being prepared by Moss Taylor.

real courage. And I still don't have the nerve or the resolve to move permanently to Cley. I don't walk down the East Bank every single day. I've certainly never looked into the eye of a godwit and wondered what lay behind its inscrutable eye. That took a completely different kind of quality – imagination.

Courage *and* imagination – now there are the co-ordinates for a life worth living.

10

The Loop, I

Bread Pudding, Nancy's, Cley,
June 1976–11 December 1988

Richard Richardson's implicit identification with the reserve at Cley throws up a number of strange and telling ironies, one of which centres on the fact that he seldom actually went on the reserve proper, but confined his activities – perhaps one should say his *inactivities* – to East Bank. This in turn may have arisen out of another irony: his poor relations with Cley's owners. There was a long, rather arcane history of disagreement between the NNT and Richard, which was perhaps more apparent than real, but which nevertheless managed to survive even his death.

After inoperable cancer carried Richard off at fifty-five, the Trust made no effort to commemorate his contribution either to the fabric of the reserve or to its general reputation as a premier bird site. Yet they did permit an independent memorial trust to dig a wetland scrape and build an associated hide on the reserve's southern perimeter. Both of these were named after the great man. There was certainly no malice aforethought intended, but to some it seemed an expression of Trust ambivalence towards him that the pool overlooked was almost permanently birdless and the Richard Richardson Hide virtually unvisited. It may conceivably have been a relief to all parties when it was knocked over by winter floods in 1996 and mysteriously disappeared thereafter.

The third and central irony attaching to Richard's identification with Cley has to do with the corresponding reputation of its old warden, Billy Bishop. Billy, son of an old north Norfolk family, inherited the job on the reserve from his father and laid the foundations of its current fame. For forty-one years Billy cleaned the dykes, cut the reeds, cleared the scrub, managed the cattle, trapped the crows, shot the foxes, dug the scrapes and endlessly manipulated water levels with a well-oiled system of cuts and sluices. Through these year-in, year-out routine practices Billy's blood, sweat and tears were literally poured into those 440 acres. In many people's eyes *he* created Cley.

If we believe in Protestant eschatology then Billy definitely went to heaven. His hard work was certainly honoured by his community. His portrait looks down in the visitors' centre. His autobiography was graced by a foreword penned by an old shooting partner, Prince Philip. If anyone truly deserved implicit association with the place it's Billy. Amongst birders, however, he's been pipped to the post by a man mainly famous for lying on his back on East Bank.

But, in a way, you've only to look at the photos of the two men in *The Birds of Norfolk* to understand the apparent anomaly. Billy stands before the reserve, a proprietorial gleam in his eye as he surveys the estate. The gun dog at his side and a walking cane in the right hand both have the appearance of slightly stagy props. So too does the pair of field glasses, the size of two small lighthouses welded together and dangling down by Billy's navel. The optics are there not exactly for watching birds, more as a symbol, gesturing that here's Billy the Birdman. Trouble is they don't really look like the equipment of a birder at all. They're more like a hunter's ancient eyepiece. Because Billy was, above everything, a poacher turned gamekeeper or, in this case, a wildfowler turned warden.

Then you look at the photo on the preceding page of a rather young Richardson in front of a Cley Heligoland trap. It's a lousy, under-exposed shot, but you can see he's not gazing aimlessly. The laser-beam vision is riveted on something, probably a bird.

Nor are the bins swinging helplessly at his belly button. They are held at chest height, immediately ready for raising to the eyes. And by comparison with Billy's they're tiny. According to Richard Mabey they were held 'between the finger and thumb of one hand, like opera glasses'. They were deliberately chosen, not to make a social point, but to be worn at all times. They were *birder's* bins. By implication they tell you why one man was remembered and the other's a sort of footnote. And that in itself, incidentally, speaks volumes about the value system inherent in birding. Creating a reserve, handling a shotgun, a tractor and a JCB are all very well. But spotting a Black Kite and nailing its identification at two miles' range – now that's something really worthy of respect.

Billy did turn up at those Richardson salons on East Bank, but sometimes it was simply to splutter derisively – curiously, Billy also stuttered – at the hero-worship that was going on. In truth he probably more often appeared not in person but as part of the conversation – as a kind authority figure, a birder's policeman, but perhaps also as a figure of fun. Because those alfresco salons were not simply ornithology's Arcadian grove. They were a forum for racy snippets of news, latest updates on running stories, a place to return to old chestnuts or to air new rumours and to invent entirely fictitious scandals. They were, in short, gossiping shops, because the patron saint of Norfolk birders also had a deliciously naughty sense of humour.

Richard Mabey recalls this aspect of the other Richard, whose performances at the East Bank salons he likened to 'a cross between Mr Punch and a weatherbeaten rocker . . .', involving 'outrageous and often libellous impersonations of other birdwatchers'.

The East Bank gatherings tell us much about the respective gap between Billy and Richard, but they also reveal something fundamental about birders in general. They *love* stories. It is, in a way, a definition of the tribe. It's a loop of tales that either binds you into the community or gently shuts you out. Of course there never has been a single cycle of stories. Each birding community has its own repertoire, whether you're from Norfolk or you're part of the Kent lot, the Cornish suppressors (only joking chaps!), the Leicester lowlisters, the Sandbach Flashers, the Wath Ings bootboys, the Upstarts, the guys at Portland Bill, the Flamborough Head team, or the Teesside crews. Each had a separate body of tales involving a specific cast of characters, but the orientation of the stories, the points being made, the issues at stake, these were common to all. In fact birding groups are amorphous and flexible. Individuals can be part of several groups, taking with them one pool of gossip into the other. Very often particularly good or important tales span the whole birding network.

The stories most often involve other birders, but they are usually shaped around an individual bird, usually a rarity. Often the anecdote will describe how someone managed to see that particular species – how they got to hear about it, the long overnight hitch they had to make, where they dossed the night before or, even, how they dipped on it. That individual bird operates like a tent pole around which a fabric of tales can be folded. And the point needs repetition. Birders may talk about birds generically, but in twitching stories it's always about particular individuals. These are then identified as such by a combination of their date or location. So it might be 'the Vorran Island Steller's' or the 'Uist Steller's' or the ''77 Franklin's' (Franklin's Gull, an American vagrant that appeared in Lowestoft) or the '76 Ross's Gull' (need I say more).

Birders can measure any stranger's credentials, his past and his web of contacts by a question-and-answer session involving a list of these key sightings. Some of them are like prized trophies or old war medals. To be able to say you saw the '62 Houbara (an Asiatic vagrant of which this was the last of just five recorded in British history) or the '66 Thrasher (Brown Thrasher is an American species that's occurred just once in Britain ever), is like admitting you own a forgotten Van Gogh. You're a figure of instant respect, fascination and envy.

It's strange to think that no one now gathers on East Bank and nothing survives of its heyday as a school for scandal. But if stories could leave physical remains that might be dug up and examined, then all the ground beneath where we used to sit would be a deep humus of forgotten anecdotes and lost yarns. I could just imagine in years to come, a couple of eager young birding archaeologists on East Bank, trowels in hand, one holding up a few half-rotted sentences, and shouting, 'Hey! What about this! Look at those long vowels, that machine-gun rattle of consonants. Must be a Norfolk accent . . . and a stutterer . . . Billy Bishop, surely?'

'Naaa!' says the other. 'Look at that long "A". South London, man, or I'm Louis Leakey's uncle. I reckon that's Richardson . . . Could be a classic . . . Remember the time he made that cut-out, painted to look like a different species on each side, which he put out on Arnold's Marsh to fool everyone. It swung in the wind a bit . . . made it look more life-like. The laughs that thing caused . . .'

Yet East Bank wasn't the only place where the stories would have heaped up. Another classic location was known as The Barn, a rickety old wooden shack just to the east of the reserve's eastern boundary. Its tin roof leaked, the old bales of straw were mouldering and the rats abundant and shamelessly bold, though the rodents were not the main reason for its celebrity. The Barn was very cheap accommodation for penniless birders. One of them even lived there for months at a stretch – a character known as Spiny Norman, a strange fellow, not simply because he went barefoot and ate coypus picked up as roadkills, but because he claimed to be so familiar with British birds he'd no need for binoculars. At weekends Spiny had to move over and share his adopted home, sometimes with over twenty young males.

I've always regretted I never saw or slept in The Barn and feel exiled from its own particular loop of tales. It strikes me as a coincidence freighted with significance that the farmer, weary of the rats, perhaps, or Spiny Norman or the crowds of young birders, pulled it down in the weeks just before I arrived. That symbolic gap in my experience marks me down as forever belonging to a later generation of Cley birders.

Yet I did experience the delights of the Beach Hotel, which is a piece of wonderful hyperbole for the weather shelter at Cley Coastguards. A typical structure of its kind, it has a square pitched roof above four separate sheltered benches each facing in a different direction. This basic accommodation, with concrete floor and completely exposed sides, was much sought after as a place to sleep. It was the obvious alternative to The Barn if you couldn't face the rats or the horseplay, and held as many as fifteen birders a night during its prime. Birders used to soothe the privations of the Beach Hotel with copious amounts of alcohol from their favourite watering hole, the George. Another small home comfort favoured by others was a sound system rigged up to the car battery from which they blasted out Seventies' progressive rock bands like Tangerine Dream at all hours of the morning. Sadly the practice of dossing there, like many of the conventions of 1970s' and 1980s' birding culture, has now largely fallen into abeyance.

Yet it has to be said that neither the Beach Hotel, nor The Barn, nor even perhaps East Bank itself can compare with another location in Cley as a place for exchange of information. The main place where birders gathered to communicate, not just with those present locally, but with birders right across the entire country, was a unique, much treasured, now long-lamented café in the village.

It was an establishment which occupied the tiny dining room in a terraced house on the left-hand side of the road as you drive east through the village. The house was called Umvolosi, an unlikely title for a Norfolk flint cottage flanked by hollyhocks. But it had apparently once belonged to a shipping manager, all of whose ships had been called after South African place names. The title had been transferred firstly from the Transvaal to his boat, then from the vessel to the house.

At first glance there seemed much that was Norfolk flint and very little that was Umvolosi about the elderly couple who owned and managed the café. Yet few would dispute that its proprietress, Nancy Gull, was an irrepressibly sunny personality, while she and her husband, Jack, operated an open-house policy in that cottage which was truly African in its communality and spirit. They were a wonderful pair. Whoever believes that a commercial enterprise cannot be an important community-building institution should have seen this café in its heyday. The place offered valuable local employment. Its fare was wholesome and unbelievably cheap. But more than that, throughout the 1970s and 1980s, until it finally closed its doors on 11 December 1988, the place was *the* central institution for Britain's birders.

Nancy's, which is what everyone called it, was legendary. Every birder knew of it. Most birders of sufficient age visited it. Many went there weekly. Some almost lived there. One or two actually did. And even those who *never* went there spoke to its occupants on a regular basis. It was routinely mentioned in that naff comedy series about birdwatching set in Liverpool called *Watching*. When the café finally closed, the event was recorded in the press and on regional and national TV. I believe it should now have one of those blue English Heritage plaques commemorating its former status.

Whenever I think of the place I am in awe of Nancy and Jack's extraordinary tolerance. The place always seemed to be open, even in midwinter, while in high summer there were sometimes thirty or forty people crammed into that tiny dining room or spilling out across rows of tables in the back garden, or sitting on the doorstep in the handkerchief-sized front garden. Often there'd be others simply waiting their turn in a long queue that trailed down the hallway.

It isn't just the crowds that make me marvel at Nancy and Jack's kindness. It was also the fact that birders are – how can I put it? – not the most sartorially elegant or domestically cultured tribe. Often we'd pile in after a rough night in The Barn or the Beach Hotel or the church porchway, unwashed, possibly soaked to the skin, occasionally covered in mud, and Nancy wouldn't

bat so much as a single eyelash. Nor did she seem to care that
we made free use of its facilities, nor the fact that birders were
often eking out a week's stay at Cley with little more than a
few quid. Nancy's fare was one of the few luxuries they could
truly afford. Her prices would have made a motorway-services
manager hyperventilate.

The pot of tea was amazing. It cost about forty pence and it
was a rare failure if you couldn't get six or seven cups from it.
People would take hours consuming these urns of liquid and
spend less than a pound. Another item on the menu that passed
into legend was the Ethelburger, a meat-based delicacy named
in honour of one of the staff, a rather crotchety, prematurely
white-haired, bent-backed Norfolk woman who addressed most
of the clientèle as 'You little bugger, you!' It was a sad day when
Ethel forsook Nancy's for a job in the local launderette.

But my all-time favourite item on Nancy's menu was her
bread pudding. About half the size of a house brick, a single
portion was in truth an entire pleasure dome by itself, comforting
in its sweetness and deliciously moist in texture. Nancy used
to make it in industrial quantities, which speaks volumes for
its popularity because one piece probably contained the daily
calorific requirements of the average adult. Two pieces were
pure excess. I used to love it so much I'd shout through to the
tiny kitchen to check she had some left even as I entered the
door. Then if it was in short supply my piece was bagged long
before any orders were taken.

The Gull family arrangements at Nancy's seemed to be based
around the café. Their children had all fledged and were never
much in evidence. Jack too, in truth, was more a presence than
a player in the running of the establishment, which is probably
why it was always known as Nancy's. When I met him he was
already white-haired and although slim and wiry managed to
appear world-worn. 'Ooh, up and down, yer know . . .' Jack
always said, whenever you enquired after his health. 'More up
than down.' Then off he'd trot to the front room to escape
the crowds with Hoopla, their rotund basset hound whose

enormously long claws rattled on the plastic runner as they made their joint escape down the hall.

For all her presiding spirit Nancy wasn't a classic matriarch. She was slight like Jack, rather frail, a dark-haired lady with a fine complexion younger than her years, a strong local accent and a high, sing-song voice and a lovely silvery, rather faltering laugh. Most regulars she knew by their Christian names. To many of us she was a blessed being, like a favourite aunt, and calling at her tiny dining room often had the atmosphere of a family visit.

But what really marked Nancy and Jack as suitable material for canonisation wasn't merely their beatific acceptance of the mud on the carpets, the furniture draped with soaking clothes and waxed cotton jackets stiff as boards, the birding paupers and the occasional hectic crowds (especially whenever a rare bird appeared at Cley Marshes) or the need to keep us all supplied with beans and eggs on toast for four, a pot of tea for three, a milky coffee and four pieces of bread pudding. Above all it was their infinite patience with the constantly ringing telephone. We complain that the phone never stops ringing if we receive perhaps a dozen calls. At Nancy's the phrase was literally, sometimes grotesquely, true. I suspect the sadists in the Soviet gulags missed a torturer's trick or two in the endlessly ringing birder's telephone.

The worst seat in the house was the one next to the phone stand because its occupant could spend the entire visit answering the same questions, sometimes every few seconds – 'Hello, can you tell me what's about?' 'Hello, can you tell me if the . . . is still there?' At a time before centrally organised rarity lines and birders' pagers, Nancy's was the key number for our information grapevine. Almost every rare sighting was entered in a logbook permanently available at Nancy's tables, and callers were either ringing to add to the daily list or, more usually, asking to know what it currently included. Towards the end, if there were no birders on the premises, Nancy took to leaving the phone off the hook. It was driving them mad.

I don't ever remember hearing the phone ring at Nancy's and it being a call for the residents of the house. It was always other birders on the line and whenever fellow birders were in the café they themselves answered it. We usually took it in turns. That way everyone got to eat while maintaining the news service. But it was essential to do so. It was part of the unspoken protocol of Nancy's and, indeed, of being a birder. Because if the loop of stories is essential to the tribe's identity, the endless loop of bird information is doubly critical. And in a way, one is a corollary of the other. They are different facets of the same oral tradition – an exchange of news which is at the heart of birding identity and culture. Just as Nancy's was the nerve centre of the communication network, it was also a place where birding stories were endlessly exchanged.

Birders had a word – *Value!* – that had nothing to do with the cost of something. It was roughly the equivalent of the Irish word *Craic*. It could imply fun, but it usually carried a kind of rough edge suggesting entertainment laced with controversy or mischief. A person could be value, a place could be value or a specific incident was value. Nancy's was value but it was also where value was endlessly retailed. Often we'd go to Cley and if there was little about bird-wise, time was divided about fifty–fifty – half in the field and half consuming one of those enormous pots of tea and soaking up the latest stories.

Nancy's was a magical place and its heyday spanned a major period in the development of British birding. Almost twenty years on from that moment at Cley, birding culture has changed almost beyond recognition. Nancy's is, of course, long closed and its wonderful owners are no more. Jack went first, followed just three years ago by Nancy herself who, tragically – especially in one who had served up such vast quantities of food for so many years – simply gave up eating. The reserve at Cley is still a wonderful setting to see birds, especially waders. The village is still a centre for bird information, home to a phone service known as Birdline, managed by two of Cley's most distinguished birder residents, Steve Gantlett and Richard Millington. And the parish probably still has more top birders per square metre than any other landscape on earth. But I think most would agree that as a location to catch the latest value Cley is no longer the centre of our universe. For me personally, this has irretrievably changed my relationship with the place.

In the science fiction film *The Matrix*, its hero Neo, played by Keanu Reeves, has to battle with a dynasty of ruthless machines in human form. As he does so he comes to terms with the fact that the real human inhabitants are simply slaves to the machines and imprisoned in a computer-generated world devised by artificial intelligence. Part of Neo's triumph over this illusory 'virtual' world is that he sees it eventually for what it is – an endless fabric of computer-generated symbols.

I see Cley in a rather similar way, not just as a beautiful and bird-enriched landscape but as a location made up by layer upon layer of stories. Its physical realities are somehow fused with an endless web of birders' words. But it is not a landscape made more vibrant by the presence of a living oral tradition. The loop of words which interlaces it is spoken by the half-faded voices of the past. It's a place of memory and ghosts and has become a kind of history book, in which I'm able to read my own past and the past of my friends. Cley is that one setting where I confront the most intriguing of all strangers – my former self.

11

The Loop, II

1 Black-winged Pratincole, Glareola nordmanni
Manor Farm Sewage Works, 7 August 1976

It's all very well getting maudlin and telling you about the oral traditions which are such a central part of the birders' world. Time, I think, to bring you into the loop, so let's set the scene.

It's Nancy's. She's in the kitchen. Jack and Hoopla have just trotted for cover in the front room. We're in the garden. The sun's shining and overhead swifts are screaming blue murder and scything the air like a bunch of black-hearted sadists. Otherwise Cley is quiet and the phone's relatively calm. The pot of tea for two is ordered and the bread pudding's on its way. In the meantime you've opted for the Ethelburger. I'm having poached egg and beans on two toast. This one's on me. So sit back and soak up the value.

Story One

1. We're in Slough Grammar School and it's 18 October 1957. This is always the peak month for bird migration and the optimum time for seeing rare birds. Ron Johns is then in his late teens and in the sixth form. He is also a budding birder with great promise but, notwithstanding the fact that by the

1970s almost every birder in full-time education was bunking off to see rarities, Ron has no thoughts of absenteeism. Besides, this is 1957, a world away from that kind of post-Wilsonian permissiveness that my generation grew up with. And in any case, the school's new headmaster, Dr Long, an austere disciplinarian Scotsman, isn't likely to be over-receptive to the idea of a Short-billed Dowitcher as an excuse for missing a history lecture. Not even when this particular transatlantic vagrant is a first for Britain.

But then Ron doesn't even know about the bird at this stage. In 1957 there's no bird grapevine to keep him informed of rarities. Most people don't even have phones. Nor does he have any transport to cover the 170 miles separating Slough Grammar from the creature in question. So as the bird settles in to probe the congenial National-Trust-owned mudflats of Salthouse in Norfolk, the young Johns listens in blissful ignorance to an account of George Trevelyan's historiographic treatment of Cromwell. However, it's at this point that his two carefully separated worlds – that of conscientious scholar and passionate birder with a hankering for rarities – begin inexorably to collide.

Midway through the lesson the head's secretary suddenly appears at the door, enters the classroom, speaks briefly with the history teacher, then requests that Johns temporarily abandon Cromwell and follow her to the head's study. Ron's completely mystified. What the hell does this mean? He racks his brains for any possible misdemeanour that might warrant Dr Long's attention and which could account for the intrusion into his schoolday routine.

At the principal's office Ron is ceremoniously ushered into the presence of Slough Grammar School's senior master and as he opens the door he notices, standing next to Dr Long, a figure who, though deeply familiar, is in the weirdest context. Ron does a double-take as he grapples with this surreal moment because there before him, in jeans, biker's boots and black leather jacket, is none other than Richard Richardson. But what the ... hell is he doing at Slough Grammar, in the headmaster's office?

Ron and Richard have been friends for years, after Ron bought a copy of Richard's field guide and saw an article about the artist and his love of the birds at Cley. After initial contact by letter, Ron makes annual pilgrimage to Cley, to take B'n'B with Mrs Davison, to join the salons on East Bank, to learn about birds and to be sponsored as a trainee bird ringer under Richard's tutelage. Richardson is, however as distant an educator as you could imagine from the model presented by the Scotsman running Slough Grammar. In fact one wonders precisely what the forbidding Presbyterian would have made of the rather louche Lee Marvin-like figure stood before him?

Apparently nothing too awful. Because Richard then announces in his customary faltering manner, 'H-h-h-h-ello, Ron. I've c-c-c-ome t-t-to take you to Norfolk to see a D-d-d-d-dowitcher.'

It transpires that Richard has got up that morning, ridden through the village, past where we're now sitting in Nancy's, and driven the three miles up the road from Cley to Salthouse to see what was then thought to be Britain's first-ever record of Short-billed Dowitcher. He's then decided that he'd like to share the pleasures of this American vagrant with his young friend. So Richard gets on his Matchless 350, roars off to Norwich, goes all the way down the A11, then round the North Circular and 170 miles later eventually arrives in Slough, where he locates the school, goes to the head's office and speaks to Dr Long, spinning him a yarn about how important it would be to the development of Ron's ornithological education that he see this particular rare species. The dour Scot is apparently convinced, probably as much by the sheer audacity of Richard's proposal as any genuine educational argument, and Ron is whisked off to Norfolk on the back of the bike to see the Dowitcher the following morning and complete one of the best, early twitching tales you'll ever hear.

There are two small footnotes:

1a The Dowitcher's location obviously made an impression on Ron because he and his wife, Sue, eventually bought a house and moved to Salthouse on 1 May 1987.

1b Years later the Salthouse 'Short-billed Dowitcher' was proved to have been a very closely related, but much commoner species, called a Long-billed Dowitcher, of which there have now been over 200 records in Britain. The first incontrovertible record of Short-billed Dowitcher didn't occur until September 1999, forty-two years after the misidentified bird. Ron and Sue drove the 535 miles to Rosehearty, Aberdeenshire to see it . . . from Salthouse.

Story Two

It's September 1975. Dick Filby – he who hitched for the Vorran Steller's – has just had an outstanding week of birding: seven superb rarities, all ticks, in eight days. It started off on the Saturday with a Crested Lark, a species that breeds as close to Britain as Calais. Yet *la Manche* seems to present an almost insuperable barrier to this widespread continental resident, since there have been only two birds in the last quarter century. Neither stayed more than seventy-two hours. Filby saw the first of these.

On the Tuesday Dick, still only a teenager, bunks off school and sets off from London with his friend Ron Johns for the Scillies. They were after three American landbirds – the Black-and-White Warbler, Scarlet Tanager and Yellow-bellied Sapsucker. It was an almost unprecedented twitch and to have seen all three has a cachet that exceeds even the '62 Houbara or the '66 Thrasher. The first two were both second records for Britain while the Sapsucker was a first for Europe (if one excludes a dead bird picked up in Iceland) and has never recurred in the UK. Dick saw all three, plus two extremely rare waders, Sociable Plover (a Russian species) and Lesser

Golden Plover (an American), one on each of the two legs of the Cornwall journey. Then on the Saturday, a week after his Dungeness Crested Lark, he heads for the Midlands for another rare transatlantic wader, a Killdeer.

Not content with a run of luck few will ever surpass, Dick heads back to the Scillies the following weekend for another American landbird, called a Bobolink. He fails on this, but enjoys a modicum of compensation in the form of a rare north-eastern European bird called Red-throated Pipit. Then at the end of his week on Scilly he hears about a couple of great birds in Norfolk, one a Radde's Warbler at Holkham Pines (the same species which Richard Richardson kept in his aviary while Ken Williamson rushed down overnight from Scotland). The other, at Blakeney Point, was a close relative, a Dusky Warbler, an Asiatic species from the genus *Phylloscopus*. Both are top rarities and Dick decides to go for them.

The carload assembling at Penzance Harbour involves the driver and car-owner Geoff, his cousin (known only to the others by his somewhat mysterious nickname, Butcher Dan), Dick himself and Dick's old friend Tim. They set off across country to cover the 350-mile journey overnight. About Oxford Geoff decides he's knackered and can Tim, who's passed his test but not driven for several months, take over at the wheel. No problem. Off they go. Geoff watches Tim for a while, decides he's fine and falls asleep.

Then, somewhere close to the Norfolk/Cambridgeshire border, Tim decides he's bored with watching the small tunnel of road and verge illuminated by the car's headlights. He decides it would be more interesting to have a one-to-one with Dick on the back seat and turns his head over his shoulder towards the seat directly behind him. As he cranes his neck round, Tim automatically twists his outstretched arms and rotates the wheel, thus turning the car sharply to the left. At seventy miles an hour, the vehicle responds in kind by mounting the left verge almost instantaneously.

At this point in the proceedings adrenalin kicks into play,

most of it gushing to the pit of Tim's stomach. He turns back immediately to address the impending crisis and responds by turning the steering wheel hard to the right. But the reaction is somewhat out of proportion to the initial action. The laws of physics, beautiful in their simplicity, are now propelling the car diagonally back across the fenland road straight for the ditch on the right-hand side.

At this moment Geoff senses he must slough off the fog of sleep and awakes to find himself careering to almost certain doom. He does the only thing possible. He wrests the wheel out of Tim's hands and attempts to right the car's trajectory. But in so doing he slews the vehicle across the road, over on to its side and they spin nose-first, upside down into the ditch.

Remember it's 1975. That felicitous piece of legislation concerning mandatory seat belts is still sometime in the future. Tim, bound neither by regulation nor safety harness, really has only one option. He punches out the windscreen with his skull and flies headlong through the shattered glass, ending up some distance away in the bottom of the ditch. Geoff avoids that fate, but whacks into the front of the car and ends up with a variety of cuts and bruises.

Dick, meanwhile, slams hard across the backseat into the sizeable frame of Butcher Dan. This close encounter is yet one more instance of fortune in Dick's luckiest of twitching runs. But their brief physical assignation, alas, is not an equal one. For while Butcher Dan has broken Dick's fall, Dick in exchange has broken Butcher Dan's collarbone and that particular piece of internal anatomy is now protruding visibly.

Perhaps we can now gain some inkling into the latter's somewhat mysterious nickname because, despite the obvious and intense pain and despite the raw vision of blood and bone, Butcher Dan now manages to lever himself out of the hazardous position in the car's interior. As he does so there's a moment of silence. The three inside the car briefly contemplate their happy fate at still being alive, while being assailed by the pungent and unmistakable odour of road accident – a blend of burnt rubber, newly mown grass, crushed metal, petrol fumes and acute fear.

Tim too, surfacing from his recent plunge through the windscreen and reflecting no doubt on the fact that he's just nearly killed them all and completely trashed Geoff's car, tries to summon a formula of words commensurate with the occasion. It comes out as, 'Sorry, Geoff, what did I do wrong?' It's offered in all innocence. Geoff responds with a due sense of fairness and proportion, 'You over-corrected, Tim.'

Given the circumstances, I'm sure you can imagine that Dick, once assured that all is (in relative terms) well, can really have only one possible thought on his mind. That's it . . . how can he get the optics out the boot and how are they going to get to see the birds?

Part of the problem is resolved by the arrival of the ambulance. All are quickly loaded aboard and taken off to King's Lynn hospital, where Dick is trolleyed in on a stretcher to X-ray. Some time later a doctor arrives on the ward, tracing his finger along the still-connected bones and joints revealed on the negative image, and finally announces (as if Dick needs to be reminded!), 'You're a very lucky man, Mr Filby.' Does he perhaps know Dick's seen the tanager, the black-and-white *and* the sapsucker? 'There's nothing wrong with you, by the looks of it. You can get dressed if you wish.'

Dick definitely does. It's about seven o'clock and getting light and the Radde's will be on view very shortly. The trouble is he's in such acute pain and so badly bruised on his shoulder that he can't actually raise his arms to dress himself. That particular problem is resolved with the help of a nurse. The question of how to hitch to Wells-next-the-Sea is addressed by Tim, who, despite his triple somersault with tuck through the windscreen, is probably the least injured of them all.

To cut a long story short, they eventually hitch the thirty miles to Wells, probably assisted by the fact that Dick presents a roadside vision of the walking wounded, and they get to the spot where the Radde's is showing. By holding his binoculars with just his one good arm and by stooping a bit, Dick manages to adjust his six-foot frame so that his eyes, his bins and the Radde's are all sort of in alignment. It's not the best possible view. But then the Radde's – small, brownish, skulking – is not visually very exciting. And in most people's eyes it certainly isn't the kind of bird to die for. But Dick, having nearly performed exactly that feat, feels he owes it to himself to behold the little fellow. And all, eventually, is well that ends well.

Story Three

It's 7 August 1976. Clive Byers – he who hitched for the Vorran Steller's with Dick Filby – has just heard about the Black-winged Pratincole that's turned up at Reading sewage farm. Pratincoles are wonderful creatures. With their long wings and tails and short stumpy legs, they rather resemble brown terns when you see them perched on the ground. But when they're airborne hawking for insects overhead, these graceful, aerobatic waders come to look more like large hirundines. Black-winged Pratincole is not only beautiful, it's also very rare. In 1976 there have been just fourteen records ever in Britain and most keen young birders had never seen one. It's a great bird to see.

There are just two small glitches with it. The first is the farmer over whose land the bird has been seen hawking. He's apparently opposed to birders going on it and has taken to some fairly radical measures in order to discourage them. But forewarned, thinks Clive, is forearmed and he's undeterred.

The other slight problem is he can't easily get a lift. But Clive's birding friend, John, has persuaded a non-birding mate to come along for the ride. Or rather, to take *them* along for a ride, because he's actually the one with the car. Unfortunately his name has passed from history, but the circumstances are quite familiar. Non-birders hear about a few of the adventures that birders get up to and, being of an adventurous nature themselves, or possibly just because they've time on their hands and want to spend a bit of it doing something completely different, they decide to give it a whirl. John's mate – let's call him Dave – is in for a whirl I doubt he's ever forgotten.

Early on a Saturday morning they all set off for Reading sewage farm, park up as instructed and set off across the fields. There's already a congregation of other birders visible on a bank some way off, who've all got to the site without crossing the land of the unco-operative farmer or, at least, having crossed it without that particular landowner knowing too much about it. Unfortunately Clive and John are unaware of any alternative route and they continue to make their way to the pratincole spot. But as they head along the path they see the farmer heading towards them in his tractor with some piece of agricultural equipment attached to the rear.

Clive and the others immediately put plan B into operation, which involves scrambling like hell down the side of the bank adjacent to the sewage farm, where they hunker down at the back of the thickest patch of bushes, hoping he hasn't seen the route of their escape. They are, they assume, invisible to the farmer, who approaches as close as he can, then stops the tractor.

All we can surmise about what happens next is that the farmer does know of their presence and more or less guesses where they must be hiding. Because after a moment's silence there is a sharp mechanical clanking, then the sound of changing gears, a revving engine and a loud, intense whirring coming from the direction of the tractor – the noise, no less, of the propelling mechanism for a muck-spreader.

The sound increases and is accompanied by a powerful torrent of liquid that penetrates the deepest defences of the two birders' (and the one non-birder's) bushy retreat. As it does so, Clive enjoys an experience which he subsequently likens to the sensation of taking a shower. Pleasant though the image may sound initially, try to imagine that this is, in fact, a cold shower. Then reflect that it is a cold shower in which you are actually fully clothed. Finally contemplate, if you will, that the viscous green fluid drenching you from head to toe is nothing less than liquefied manure.

All of this sounds bad enough for Clive and John, but there is one further layer of misery which is reserved for Dave alone. Remember he's not gone along because he's a birder. He probably couldn't give a toss about seeing the Black-winged Pratincole. Nor is there the smallest crumb of comfort in the idea that it's going to make a hell of a good story to tell the boys.

No. Strange though it may seem, given the fact that their ultimate destination is a sewage farm, Dave's only real reason for going to Reading is to have a bit of a laugh with his mates. Instead, here he now stands drenched to the bone in diluted pigshit.

But let's not get too downhearted. This is ultimately a tale of the birder's triumph over adversity, a spirit that now fills Clive, John and possibly even Dave, because as they climb out the hollow, stinking and bedraggled, the forty birders securely positioned on the distant bank start to clap and cheer and raise their telescopes in salute to the doughty trio.

Clive and the others really feel that having been completely caked in shit they have nothing to lose by confronting the farmer in person ... well, nothing to lose, that is, except their lives. Because the lunatic with the muck-spreader has now gone completely ballistic with a spanner and stands there, face bright purple, screaming every kind of rustic profanity in the Berkshire farmer's canon. Clive and John, as you can imagine, really have only one thought on their mind. How can they get round this frothing maniac and over to the bank where the bird's showing.

They decide to leg it over the fields and get to the spot where their friends and colleagues are standing, who renew their applause and congratulations. Then, ignoring the rich odour emanating from their persons and through the haze of manure drying on their bins, Clive, John and Dave drink down the refreshing, the lovely, the graceful, the very rare form of Britain's fourteenth Black-winged Pratincole.

3a There is a delightful, if rather pungent, footnote to Clive and John's tale of the Reading Black-winged Prat (as it would normally be called).

They and their chauffeur, Dave, finally get back to the car and head off up the M4, no doubt reflecting on their little adventure, but hardly realising that it hadn't quite ended. Because shortly afterwards the car breaks down and while managing to nurse it off the motorway, they were unable to complete their home run in the vehicle and Clive and John finally have to catch a bus. Can you imagine?

I see them getting on and, at about the point when the bus driver gives them their change and tickets, the odour starts to kick in. By the time they reach their seats it pervades the entire vehicle. Everyone else looks at the two young men wearing bins and scope, soaked to the skin on a perfectly pleasant day, and wonders whether the stink and their simultaneous arrival are related events. Kids begin to snigger. Those who manage to sneak a closer look can see that both of them have their hair plastered down by a hardening green-brown cap and all across their cheeks, forehead and neck are little runnels and teardrops of a congealed brown liquid.

Two old ladies, complete with purple rinse and bucket handbags on lap, sit directly behind Clive and John. Screwing up their faces and turning to each other, one says, 'Oh my goodness, Mrs Arbuthnot, dear, somebody *has* been muck-spreading today!'

These are just three examples from an almost endless canon of birders' tales. They offer a brief insight into birding culture but, before we finish the last of our seven cups of tea and settle the bill with Nancy, there are a couple of questions I want to address. How important are these stories to birders and, also, how important are they to me as a birder? I think the best way I can answer the questions is to finish with another little tale.

In the late 1980s I saw in my own and other birders' obsessions with travel something that seemed to reflect a national preoccupation. Drawing on these personal experiences, I began writing a book about the British people's longstanding love affair with travel and travel writers, which was eventually published as *Loneliness and Time*. During the course of the project I wrote to and was granted an interview by the great post-war explorer, Arabist and photographer, Wilfred Thesiger, author of two classic travel works, *Arabian Sands* and *The Marsh Arabs* (not to forget a short paper in *The Ibis* on Ethiopian birds).

On the appointed day I called at his Chelsea flat and when he came to the door he opened proceedings by thrusting his hand out in the conventional manner. I attempted to respond in kind, only to find myself grappling with what seemed like a huge stump of oak. I felt like applying both hands and digging in my nails so that I might make at least some kind of physical impression on the inert mass.

I was ushered into his spacious drawing room, with its exotic mementoes from sixty years of continuous African and Asian wanderings: beautiful eastern carpets and kilims, horn-handled daggers, late-nineteenth or early-twentieth-century images of the Orient, bookcases of rare travel volumes. I set up my little recorder and prompted the great man with a set of questions about his historic journeys across the Empty Quarter.

I was just thirty, nervous, rather formal. Thesiger, who was already about eighty, was perfectly at ease, lolling in his chair, casually flicking worry beads back and forth as if they were a kind of aide-mémoire to his days in the East. I remember at one point some BBC producer rang in the middle of our discussions. From one half of the conversation, and from Thesiger's increasingly clipped tone, I inferred that he was nonchalantly turning down a request for a televised interview with the casual precision that one might apply to squashing a particularly troublesome insect.

After a range of questions we eventually got round to Thesiger's deep affection for the lifestyle of the Bedu, whose nobility he couldn't emphasise more strongly. They were a tribe, he said, whose traditions went back to the very origins of civilisation. One thing he held in awe was the extraordinary strength of their oral traditions. The tale I remember most clearly concerned his party's emergence from the Rub al Khali after their historic crossing of this desolate region. The small group was later reunited with the rest of Thesiger's entourage, most of whom were related to one another and members of the Rashid tribe.

'And do you know how long they discussed our crossing of the Empty Quarter?' Thesiger asked, as we moved towards the moral of this particular story. 'It would have taken me about four hours to describe the whole thing. But they discussed everything we did in the most minute detail. They talked about it for four days!'

I got the picture that astonishment was called for and raised my eyebrows, held up my hands and let out a long audible whistle of incredulity. But I have to confess, I'm afraid I wasn't in the slightest bit impressed. I chuckled inwardly and felt rather like Crocodile Dundee when he's faced with the stiletto-wielding mugger in New York. 'That's not a knife,' Dundee says, '*this* is a knife!' And he pulls out that saurian-slaying cleaver from his back pocket.

Wilfred Thesiger is one of the most extraordinary and impressive human beings I've met, but on that point I reckon I could have trumped his tale easily. There was any number of birding stories I could have recounted. But the edit-room rewrite I composed later in my head ran something like this: 'Do you know what, Mr Thesiger? I went to Nepal with my mate, Alan Adams from Liverpool – you know, the guy who helped find Britain's first Eleonora's

Falcon? Do you know how long we talked about other birders? Four months! FOUR WHOLE MONTHS! . . . without stopping. Now there's an oral tradition that's *really* worth celebrating.'

12

545 and 514

1 adult male Pallas's Sandgrouse, Syrrhaptes paradoxus
Loch Spiggie, Shetland, 19 May 1990

On the face of it Ron Johns doesn't strike you as the sort of man to feature too often in the birders' loop of tales. He looks a rather mild, unassuming sort of fellow, bespectacled, trim in figure, neat in dress, with a verbal style that suggests his words and thoughts are chosen with deliberation. Not the sort, for sure, to spark controversy or invite speculation.

But Ron's probably featured as regularly and prominently in the tribe's cycle of stories as any other living birder. I'd certainly heard of him by the time I was fourteen, almost thirty years ago. Though it'll amuse him and embarrasses me to admit it, I've discussed and reflected on Ron's achievements on numerous occasions. My guess is that hundreds of other birders might be left a touch bashful should they read this. Truth is, we've *all* talked about him, even if, like myself, we barely know him. But then Ron is a phenomenon, a legend, a seemingly permanent stellar fixture in the birding firmament.

His achievement is simple. He's seen more birds in the British Isles than any other person, past or present. In this country he was probably the third man ever to see 300, the first to 400, then 500 species, and he will soon achieve 550. It's less likely he'll be the first to reach 600. In the rarefied

117

atmosphere surrounding Britain's top listers a handful of new birds a year is all they can hope for. For Ron, time's simply running out. Equally significant is the fact that, in keeping with the persona of moderation and self-control, Ron recently declared his *semi*-retirement from the field of British listing to focus on foreign birding. Yet his current total list of 545 species (at the last count) represents over 90 per cent of the total number of birds ever recorded in these islands in the last two centuries. No doubt one day it will be surpassed, but it will be virtually impossible for anyone ever to hold the title for the length of time that Ron's maintained his own position. He's been number one for over thirty-three years.

How can I convey the extraordinariness of that 545 to a non-birder? Sporting analogies are the most obvious comparison. It's like Steve Redgrave winning the gold for rowing over eight successive Olympics. It's the equivalent of Steve Davis going back to Sheffield's Crucible for three decades and retaining the world championship each year. It's like Manchester United taking the Premiership title every season until 2020. It should sound amazing. It might also sound a bit boring (given the last analogy even Ron might think so: he's a fanatical Liverpool fan). But the truth is birders have never known anything else. Ron's been there for ever. This chapter is about how he managed it and a fraction of what it entailed.

The foremost factor to explain that size of bird list is the sheer length of Ron's birding career. Although he wears his sixty years as lightly as his birding crown, he was there when the proto-twitcher first emerged from the primeval slime way back in the 1950s. In fact his first ever *serious* twitch was before the word had been coined – the occasion when Richard rolled up at Slough Grammar on his Matchless 350 to take Ron for the Short-billed Dowitcher. While we now know it was, in fact, merely another record of its sibling species, the Long-billed Dowitcher, we can easily forgive him. The young Johns had got going long before the development of all the literature and paraphernalia and expertise which makes current bird identification such a seriously high-tech affair.

In fact he recalls tricky moments in the early days when the bird i.d. process included eliminating the insect that was just then walking across one of the internal prisms on his bins. There were also rain-affected seawatches when hi-tech optical maintenance involved unscrewing the object lens and pouring the water out of the bottom. It sounds so long ago I can only envisage it in sepia tones, but the fact that Ron was there *then* is among the reasons he's number one *now*.

His birding began in fairly conventional style: a brief flirtation with collecting eggs, a copy of *The Observer's Book of Birds*, outings with a local wildlife group – the Middle Thames Natural History Society – childhood visits to the local woods and reservoirs. Another routine feature was tutelage from a birding elder. The difference between Ron and most of us is that he got it straight from the top. From 1955 onwards his birding mentor was Richard Richardson. The two were close friends for over twenty years; Richard was godfather to Ron's son and Ron was one of the last people ever to see the great man alive. As his friend was waning in October 1977, Ron went to visit him at Kelling Hospital in north Norfolk. Only the day before Ron had come off Fair Isle. As poignant and telling a vision of our tribe and its ethos is the last image of the two of them, Richard propped up in bed, discussing the Pechora Pipit and Great Snipe that had just been seen on his favourite Scottish island as his life ebbed away. He died that same night.

The fact that Ron was going from the late 1950s also meant that he saw most of those early classic birds about which we mere mortals can only fantasise. Needless to say, it includes both the '62 Houbara and the '66 Thrasher I mentioned earlier. The first of these was an extraordinary creature. Of the five individuals seen in British, four were in the nineteenth century and the bird that turned up almost forty years ago in east Suffolk was the last.★

With Houbara it's not just the bird's rarity value. The beast is also strikingly beautiful. Like most members of the bustard family it's a large turkey-sized creature that has the long legs and long neck of a ground-dwelling species. Wild and wary, its normal strategy when threatened is to run away at speed, or crouch down sometimes with neck stretched flat along the ground, when it relies on the subtle crypsis of its complex plumage to protect it. While we can hardly hope to observe the behaviour in Britain, the male's breeding display is a piece of sexual theatre fit to make the gods laugh.

He has elongated black and white plumes on the sides of his throat and breast, which he raises up and spreads out while simultaneously retracting the crown into his neck. This action causes the eye, beak and face – literally the whole head – to vanish beneath a shaggy white ruff. The posture combines exaggerated style with bizarre humour – a surreal blend of regency fop with some decapitated creature off *The Muppets*. As if that weren't sufficiently absurd, the 'headless' bird then trots along with a high prancing step while zigzagging from side to side. Occasionally these swaggering but essentially blind sorties end up with the bird crashing into a bush or stone like a drunken idiot.

★ There's an interesting postscript to the '62 Houbara, as I shall persist in calling it. Yet perhaps I ought not, because in the late 1990s it was decided that the two races of the bird, one inhabiting the deserts of North Africa and the other spread across Asia from Sinai to Mongolia, should be elevated to the status of two separate species. On the basis of this taxonomic split, the Suffolk bird, which was a representative of the Asian population, should technically become a MacQueen's Bustard. However the old name is so indelibly rooted in birding lore it's difficult to think of it as anything other than the '62 Houbara. But it does mean that, were the North African bustard to appear in Britain, the one still called Houbara, then Ron could tick this wonderful bird all over again.

Another classic early bird that identifies Ron as an old-timer, but explains why he's number one, is the Hartlepool Dusky Thrush – a Siberian species of which there have been just eight. It turned up in the winter of 1959–60, but Ron only heard about it when a friend from Middlesbrough happened to mention it in a letter. By the time he decided to bear the expense and take the train north – forty-nine shillings for the return ticket – the bird had already been there six weeks. True to his reputation for luck – some of his friends knew him as 'Horseshoe' Johns – Ron not only found the thrush hopping around on the seafront, but he got another new species in a Little Auk offshore. It was two pounds nine shillings well spent. There's only been one other twitchable Dusky since and that bird was on Shetland.

In birding parlance the Dusky Thrush is known as a 'blocker'. It's a rare bird that a few *have* seen but most *haven't*. Its status as a blocker isn't immediately apparent. Only with the passage of years and the failure of another individual to appear in Britain, do people begin to realise the chances of seeing that particular species have effectively become 'blocked up'. Conversely to see one of these blocked birds or a bird which, for personal reasons, you as an individual have not had an opportunity to see, is to *unblock* it. (That's why Richard Millington, in his *Twitcher's Diary*, talks about finally unblocking the Steller's Eider.) Yet some birds like the Hartlepool Dusky, the '62 Houbara and the '66 Thrasher, have never been unblocked. It was by seeing exactly these species that Ron stole such a vital lead on all his rivals.

But to get a big list isn't just about starting young and having some luck. The three species just mentioned are known as *long-stayers*, birds which hang around for weeks or even months. In fact in the early days all the rarities seen by a relatively wide cross-section of birders had to be long-stayers almost by definition. The haphazard and virtually incidental chains of communication amongst Britain's birders meant that it took weeks for people to hear about such rarities and, often, equally long periods to find the opportunity to go to see them.

This couldn't contrast more sharply with today's scene, when birders can subscribe to one of the two paging services, Bird Alert and BirdNet. These information systems supply virtually minute-by-minute updates on the whereabouts and behaviour of specific rarities. Otherwise you can ring the Cley-based phone service on national rarities, Birdline, or one of the half-dozen regional bird information networks. Today, as you make your journey to Hartlepool, almost every inch of the way you can be in touch with the bird's movements. All of this can make Ron's early efforts seems rather amateurish, but that disguises a different kind of quality without which you can't really account for his number one status. I can best explain it by telling the story of another rarity.

The 1970s were, in a sense, the start of a new phase in Ron's birding career. By that time he was already conscious of his number one status and, therefore, that he had a record to protect. Equally, in the previous year he had made the first of an eventual 100-plus birding trips abroad. But on 2 May 1970 it was Ron's thirtieth birthday. He was celebrating with friends in the George at Cley, a pub just across the road from Nancy's and the other great recycling centre for birders' stories, value and gen. In fact at that time it eclipsed Nancy's as the centre of the grapevine, people ringing in and out from the pub all the latest sightings. On that particular Saturday evening, as the grapevine networked across the country, someone happened to ask Ron what he'd really like as a birthday present.

Naturally what he wanted most was another of those mythic birds, which he knew then as Indian Tree Pipit. It's familiar today as Olive-backed Pipit but let's retain the old name, which is such a powerful feature of its original allure. The hippie trail to the East was in full swing and all things Indian seemed wreathed in mystery. This beautiful but elusive and little-known pipit was the birder's object for this oriental fascination. (I must declare a more personal attachment to the bird, which is expressed partly through its Latin patronymic *Anthus hodgsoni*. The person after whom the species is named is Brian Hodgson. This remarkable, nineteenth-century polymath, now largely forgotten – yet in his day educated by Malthus, a correspondent of Darwin, an uncle by marriage to the early socialist Beatrice Webb, a founder of the Western study of Tibetan Buddhism, a pioneer anthropologist, a minor Anglo-Indian politico and a giant of Himalayan natural history – was the subject of a first co-authored book.)

In May 1970 Britain had seen just three examples of *Anthus hodgsoni*. Ron wanted number four. Within minutes of expressing his fantasy wish, some character came on the phone reporting a rumour that was doing the rounds on an Indian Tree Pipit which might have been seen at Portland in Dorset earlier that day. Because of the weird coincidence it was initially dismissed as a joke, but Ron and his mates rang round their own extensive contacts to see what they could find out. Even so, little more was forthcoming and when Ron got up at eleven o'clock, undaunted by the lack of news, and announced they were going there and then for the bird, his companions initially thought this was a second wind-up. It was only when Ron started dismantling his tent towards midnight that they all realised he was in earnest.

So through the night they drove the 250 miles from north Norfolk to Portland and arrived the next dawn to discover that only two other keen birders of the day had heard and made the effort to follow up the story. Yet they also learnt that the tally of *Anthus hodgsoni* records in Britain had indeed risen to four when an individual was seen, caught and ringed the previous day. Against expectations, since the species is notoriously skulking and often difficult to find, the bird was relocated and Ron's party saw and even photographed it.

The moral of the piece? Well, it's not the fallibility of the grapevine. Lapses like that were to be expected in a network that relied so heavily on the personal contact. No, the key point is Ron's drive and nerve to take that sort of risk and make his own luck. He'd created opportunity almost from nothing. It deserves a special kind of credit.

There is a side issue which I have to tackle before returning to the rest of the story. It has to do with the recurrent perception amongst many birders that the 1960s and 1970s were the golden age of twitching. There are a number of elements at work in this sense of nostalgia, but one that the Indian Tree Pipit story illustrates perfectly is the risk of failure.

Distilling intelligence on rare bird sightings was itself an intensely social and essentially socially creative process, but it was an inexact art. Often one went blind on a hunch. And it was precisely the degree of uncertainty which edged one's expectations with a sense of excitement. It meant you could easily *dip* – the birder's term which describes the associated crash in spirits when you fail to find the bird. But it also meant that fulfilling the half-promised goal could be tinged with a magical thrill. It was like plucking joy from thin air.

Perversely, I suspect twitching declines in satisfaction with a reduction, not in the chances of *seeing* the bird, but of *missing* it. The problem is that today's technology is narrowing that margin of error. If we finally achieve what amounts to a guarantee of success, then we will have reduced this wonderful pastime to the mechanistic timetabled drudgery of the ultimate anoraks' pursuit – train-spotting.

Apologies for the digression because I can already hear the questions mounting up. Issues like 'How on earth did he find time to do all that chasing around?' 'Did he do any work?' 'Where was the money coming from?'

Work, in fact, is seldom a major barrier to the keen twitcher. Keeping to someone else's schedule and weekday timetable inevitably involves a certain amount of dipping. Most people can accommodate that kind of restraint. But Ron was doubly blessed in this department, because he had an excellent job, a management career with an internal consultancy to British Gas. He also worked for the same man for twenty-five years – long enough for superiors and workmates to develop understanding for their birding colleague. Taking the odd day off at short notice was never a problem if the schedule permitted. And while time may have been at something of a premium, money was not. Ron could afford to fly, which was often the only way to get to the kinds of destination where a top birder needs to go. A weekend away from London on Scilly or Shetland was nothing exceptional in the Johns' household.

The problematic relationship for a twitcher isn't usually to the boss, but to your spouse, if you have one at all. Many keen birders never marry, probably for that reason. But Ron did, twice, and had children. In his second wife, Ron received the ultimate twitcher's benediction. Sue isn't only tolerant of her husband's foibles, she's a birder herself. Ron and Sue are a team and maintaining the list is a family affair, which makes it difficult to compete with that kind of mutual support and synergy. In fact nobody can. Not only does Ron have the top British bird list, Sue is the female number one with a list of 514 species. This makes it sound a little easy. But here's a final story from the Johns family album, which should tell you as much as anything about Britain's most remarkable twitching double act and the complications that birds can bring to an ordinary couple's lives.

The bird in question needs a lengthy introduction. It's a creature called Pallas's Sandgrouse, a member of an essentially desert-dwelling family that combines the basic full-chested shape of a pigeon with the subtle patterning of a gamebird. The male is a gloriously attractive beast. Except for a dove-grey pencil line from crown to mantle his evenly contoured head and neck are orange-ochre. That pleasing colour is offset by a double mayoral chain – a broad gorget of soft grey bordered by a narrower, more intense chest band of black lines upon white. The camel-coloured back and wings are broken by regular lateral stripes of brown-black, while this same colour forms a rectangular block around the lower belly. The feet and short legs are sheathed entirely in white down that has the appearance of a pair of woolly stockings. It's a ground-dwelling species and has a low-slung centre of gravity, while the body tapers at the rear to a series of long dark pins on the central tail feathers and, uniquely for a sandgrouse, on the outermost primaries.

The subtle crypsis of this desert plumage only half explains the appeal of a Pallas' Sandgrouse. The other dominant feature is the unpredictable pattern of its distribution. Normally it comes no closer to Europe than a broad belt of arid steppe from Kazakhstan to Manchuria. However, climatic fluctuations across the inner Asian range occasionally trigger a mass exodus of Pallas's Sandgrouse both to the south-east and south-west. These eruptive movements can bring the bird as far as Western Europe, although the last major influxes were as long ago as 1863, and again in 1888–9, with a final few in 1908. Since that date there has only been a scattering of singletons, each staying no more than a few days. So seeing a Pallas's Sandgrouse in the late twentieth century was a once-in-a-lifetime opportunity. That chance came on Saturday 19 May 1990.

It all started with a group of four birders who were doing a sponsored daylist in Shetland on behalf of a conservation organisation. Essentially, it's a bit of fun that involves getting friends to back you with a fixed sum for each species sighted. The more species you see in the allotted twenty-four hours, the more cash you raise for charity. But all went gloriously wrong the moment the team stopped off at Loch Spiggie, near the southernmost tip of Shetland and bumped into the only twitchable Pallas's Sandgrouse for eighty years. It was a historic moment.

Amongst their first reactions was to get the news out so that others could share the thrill of this magical bird. At that time the only major birders' information network was the Cley-based Birdline run by Steve Gantlett and Richard Millington. So they rang Steve from Shetland, Steve rang his friend Ron in the adjacent village of Salthouse and by eight o'clock that morning, just minutes after the Pallas's had first been spotted, they were already planning how to get there.

Directly door-to-door, Cley to Loch Spiggie was a cool 1450-mile round trip. In American or, perhaps, even in Australian terms, that length of journey is nothing. US twitchers routinely fly coast to coast for really big rarities. But there is a cultural context we need to take into account. Across the Atlantic, long-distance flights are cheap and routine. In Britain they're infrequent and expensive. In terms of speed and its triumph over distance and inconvenience, Ron and Steve's twitch for the sandgrouse was one of the biggest in UK birding history.

All birders want to see a Pallas's Sandgrouse. The differences between us lie in the amount of effort we expend to do so. Like me some wouldn't leave their region to see such a bird. Others probably wouldn't leave the county. That doesn't in any way reflect on our status as committed birders; seeing rarities is just not a high enough priority.

Keen twitchers will go as far as Shetland, but they will allow their immediately scheduled slate of responsibilities to continue as normal – going to work all that week, taking the kids swimming as promised, meeting their parents for the birthday meal arranged weeks before – until the opportunity to make the journey becomes feasible. But for the very top twitchers it's the extent to which they are prepared to put ordinary life on hold *instantly* for the sake of seeing that wanted bird, which distinguishes them. Yet circumstances can conspire to foil even the keenest. On this occasion Sue was blocked by work commitments.

Ron, however, could go with Steve, but the only possible way to see the bird that weekend was to fly directly to Shetland from Heathrow. Once reservations were made, there was the small preliminary business of the drive to the airport. That is, it would have been a small preliminary business had it just been a case of 170 miles at top speed. Slightly more inconvenient was the sudden, disastrous loss of a clutch less than halfway through the journey. By sheer good fortune the breakdown occurred close to a car-hire firm and, with a little running and slightly more expense than anticipated, they were soon well into plan B. This involved abandoning Steve's vehicle at the roadside and driving hell for leather to the airport in a hire car.

By about midday they arrived at Heathrow, only to find another minor obstacle. The original flight booking had been made by Ron, but he and Steve had roped in a mutual friend, who had then made his own separate booking for the same flight. At the check-in desk, however, while British Airways had registered this friend's independent reservation, there were no details on seats for Ron and Steve. While *he* could go, *they* could not. When the barrier arm came down to prevent them boarding and, for all they knew, from seeing what might be the only Pallas's Sandgrouse in their lifetimes, it was not a happy parting. But this is a story with a happy ending. Eventually they were allowed on to the plane.

Towards mid-afternoon, following a stopover in Aberdeen, all three of them – about half the total of mainland birders to reach Shetland that day – could step out of the airport on Shetland, take a deep breath, and feel the first bluffs of cold air that nag eternally at the Northern Isles. They could, at last, let go a fraction and adjust into the day's crowning moments. It was a relatively straightforward business now to be driven by a waiting friend the few miles to Loch Spiggie and roll up at the pinpointed location. It was about six o'clock in the afternoon. They'd set off at nine that morning.

There, before them, looking down his telescope was none other than the late Bobby Tulloch. During his long career, Bobby had become well known to thousands of people through wildlife lectures on his native archipelago, delivered the length and breadth of Britain. But he was also a passionate conservationist, radio presenter, film-maker, author, photographer, raconteur, living legend and top birder. Who better to make the formal introduction, to announce to you in that softly spoken dialect of the Shetlands, after a journey of a thousand miles, costing several hundred pounds – a twitch unprecedented in terms of distance and speed – for one of the most sought-after dream birds on the British list, 'Here it is . . . have a look down my scope.'

I have an inkling of what the bird meant to the three

observers. All vagrant birds, especially the rarest, are in a sense more than living creatures. Because so many birders share the same experience – in the case of the sandgrouse about 800 made the journey to Shetland – they are also a type of communal rite reconnecting you to a tribal tradition. The process operates through space and across time. On seeing a rare bird I often feel connected by the schedule of previous records to all those historic observers who have shared in the pleasures of that particular bird, lives that stretch back into the early nineteenth century and even beyond. In the case of the sandgrouse there is a web of connection all the way back to the legend of this remarkable bird's remarkable discoverer, the eighteenth-century German naturalist and explorer, Peter Pallas.

For the three English observers watching the Pallas's Sand-grouse on the evening of 19 May 1990, some, if not all, of these mental delights should have been the culmination and end of their extraordinary journey. For Steve it surely was. Yet for Ron, really, how could it be? He was going home having seen a mythic bird, but that created its own situation. Not much fun in the Johns' household if one had seen such a creature yet the other had not. Work responsibilities had prevented Sue from making the journey that weekend, but that wasn't the end of the matter. The key issue was not missing her husband's odyssey, but whether the bird would remain at Loch Spiggie until the following weekend. Luckily it did. Sue could go herself.

So the next Friday night, both of them set off to drive the 500 miles to Aberdeen. The following morning Ron waved Sue off on her flight to Shetland. Twenty-four hours later she was back. In seeing the bird herself, Sue had joined in all the meaning of its occurrence. She could also, in a way, complete Ron's own sense of satisfaction at seeing it. Pallas's Sandgrouse had become a shared pleasure in the Johns' household.

That Sunday evening, after they had returned home, they could think finally about relaxing. That is, they could think about relaxing once Sue had flown all the way back to Aberdeen, there to meet Ron, and then driven the 500 miles back down to

Norfolk. It had been a long week. Mercifully, the following day was a Bank Holiday Monday. Time and space, you might think, to put the feet up, perhaps get down the bird books and absorb a little on the remarkable creature they had just witnessed.

At ten o'clock this weary but contented birding pair, a now off-duty and essentially ordinary couple, had just got into bed . . . Then the telephone rang . . . It was Steve Gantlett . . . Some strange character had rung him up and said he was 95 per cent certain he'd just seen an Ancient Murrelet on the island of Lundy.

In 1990 I couldn't even pronounce Ancient Murrelet, let alone knew what it was. It is conceivable that even Ron and Sue hadn't a clue. But we were all just about to find out. This extraordinary little beast is a small auk, a relative of the Puffin, inhabiting the Pacific coasts of the north-western United States. It had never been recorded before in Britain. It had no great magical allure for any British birder, because no one in their wildest dreams had ever conceived such an unlikely vagrant, whose shortest journey to Britain was about 7000 miles, could ever possibly arrive on these shores. Miraculously it had. Many consider it now *the* bird of the decade, eclipsing even the sandgrouse.

It certainly presented an interesting situation in the Johns' household that evening. They'd just had an exhausting and thrilling weekend in northernmost Scotland. One of them had covered about 1500 miles and between them, they'd driven well over 1000 miles in the last three days. Altogether, over the whole two-weekend period, they'd covered about 3200 miles north and south.

Lundy, meanwhile, is a three-mile long island in the Bristol Channel lying about twenty-four miles due west of Ilfracombe. It involves about a 600-mile round daytrip from Norfolk. Beautiful and remote, it can be an absolute swine to get on and off because of the awkward schedule of the boats and the risk of being stranded by bad weather. I know what I'd have done after that message. I'd have got out the book on Ancient

Murrelet (pronounced with two syllables, incidentally, *Muir-let*), flipped through it and then placed it back on the shelf, switched off the light and enjoyed long, fulfilling dreams about Pallas' Sandgrouse.

But then I'm not Britain's number one. Ron and Sue got up, worked out the best way of getting to Bideford in Devon on a Bank Holiday Monday then set the alarm . . . very early.

13

Songs of Praise

1 adult Ancient Murrelet, Synthliboramphus antiquus
Lundy, Devon, 27 May 1990

For most birders there is only one thing better than seeing good
birds. You can probably guess what it is . . . it's actually finding
the thing for yourself. In fact for some people finding rarities is
the *raison d'être* of their birding selves. That act of independent
discovery has been elevated almost to the status of a principle,
which often forms the basis of opposition to twitching. Some
argue that without those who go faithfully to watch the same area
day in, day out, in the hope they might find something unusual,
no rare birds would ever be discovered. Twitchers, by contrast,
are viewed as parasitic upon the endeavours of these other honest
ornithological toilers, who are known as 'patch-workers'.

I'm not sure the argument is valid. The fact is that many
birders both twitch others' rarities *and* also work a local patch
themselves. After all, the two things are not mutually exclusive.
In fact they are in many ways interdependent. Finding rarities is
enormously satisfying, but if we're honest a major part of the
thrill is the kudos derived from our peers' metaphoric thumbs
of approval. Without the rare bird being found there would
certainly be no twitch. But then without the twitch there can
be no glory or, at least, much less glory.

My other objection to any moral grading of the two experiences is that finding your own rare birds is itself hardly an act

of world-saving significance. The truth is neither twitching nor finding rarities is intrinsically important. The birds themselves are disoriented vagrants which have no value in any wider ecological context. They play no part in issues of conservation and are peripheral to environmental politics, which are mainly concerned with the birds most numerous in Britain either as breeding or wintering populations. The conservation of Britain's four million Skylarks and nine million Blackbirds is important to us all. Or it should be. The value of rarities is merely the value that birders pour into them.

That, however, is massive. All birders want to find them. It's one of those defining characteristics, like walking down East Bank or wanting to see a Pallas's Sandgrouse. You could be a dude or a scientist, but if you're not bothered about finding rarities you can't really be a birder. Finding a rarity is that throat-drying, breath-snatching, chest-clutching, stomach-churning, heart-thumping, hand-trembling moment we all dream about. In birding terms it has no equal.

I must confess, my own career in the rarity-finding department is fairly modest – about a dozen significant records at most. Yet they are all still cherished memories for me, perhaps none more so than my first ever. It was at Spurn on 11 April 1974. The bird was a Hoopoe, one of those strange long-billed, long-crested creatures, whose mixture of salmon pink and pied zigzag markings adds a hint of exoticism to any Mediterranean landscape. I was with Tog and another friend when we disturbed it from the beach where it had been feeding. Off it flew, a mellifluous rolling action, a bird that resembled a gigantic butterfly, wings a strobe-light display of black and white. Such sudden and unexpected beauty was greeted firstly by a volcanic outburst of swearing, then a delirious whoop of excitement when we realised what it was.

Although it was *our* first Hoopoe and *our* first 'rare' bird, I have to admit the species doesn't really constitute a rarity. It's merely an uncommon migrant in Britain, although we sought to give it significance by describing it later to friends as the first

Hoopoe for Humberside. The fact that the county had only come into existence with that year's local government shake-up was neither here nor there.

Most of my rarities have been like that. Not simply firsts, but firsts in some speciously contrived context, or perhaps with unfortunate qualifying conditions. Typical was my Dusky Warbler, a dull brown species from east of the Urals in Russian Siberia. I saw it at Holkham in north Norfolk on 22 May 1985. All the other thirty-two records for the county have been in autumn. Mine was singing and the only spring record.

Equally unconvincing was the Black Bush-Chat I 'found' in Israel in 1981. Tog, another friend John Eames and I discovered it just to the north of the Red Sea port of Eilat. Unfortunately, no field guide of the day illustrated what is essentially a Saharan species and we hadn't the slightest clue what it was. When we returned home it was John who nailed the bird's identity, worked out it was a first for the Western Palearctic and published the record. I was mentioned in despatches, but it's not quite the same.

I suppose I shouldn't forget here my three first new species for Benin. But then again, Benin! Who the hell knows where it is? Who, even less, has ever been there? No. What you want is a nice clean straight first for Britain, seen and identified by you, enjoyed subsequently by thousands of other grateful birders, then written up by you for the two statutory vetting bodies, the *British Birds* Rarities Committee and the British Ornithologists' Union Records Committee, unanimously accepted by them both and finally published in the relevant publications.

I know exactly the bird I want to find and even where I want to find it. It'll be an Audouin's Gull at Blakeney Point or, possibly, on Arnold's Marsh off East Bank. It's now just a question of it actually happening.

While I wait for the pipe dream to come to pass I console myself with the knowledge that finding a first is statistically improbable not just for me but for everyone. There are thousands of keen birders in Britain and the candidate list of new species for these islands is about fifty, possibly a hundred at the outside. Most of us must be reconciled to a life never quite fulfilled.

But for the blessed few it can be a life-changing experience. I can recall vividly an American birder describing to me the day she found the US's first Collared Plover in Texas. When her hands rose to cover her eyes, glistening with a fresh film of moisture, she confessed that it was the greatest, happiest day of her life. If one had such things as a coats of arms or a *Who's Who* entry, then a first would feature prominently in both.

For others the bird becomes a kind of leitmotif or a symbol of themselves, to be reproduced in business cards and on letter-headed notepaper. At home, walls are adorned with photographs or paintings of the beast, and the day on which they found it is commemorated like a wedding anniversary. My guess is that if you were criminally inclined you could access certain birders' bank accounts simply by trying out as a password the English or scientific name of the species they found.

All firsts are firsts, although, sadly, not all firsts are equal. If you're going to find one, try to ensure it meets certain conditions. Best, for instance, to let others know quickly so they can share in the experience. Most people, in fact, want to proclaim the discovery to the world as loudly as possible because the real buzz is the gathering torrent of acclaim which pours your way. Although single-observer birds are no less valid as additions to the British list, they obviously lack the impact of the full-blown mass-spectator experience. And sometimes those finding a first observed *only* by themselves can discover that a little cloud envelops the record and small puffs of half-humorous innuendo amalgamate over time to produce a definite and freshening force-five slur.

It's for something like these reasons that Mark Golley, a top birder himself and former assistant warden at Cley, defines the twenty minutes after quarter past six on the evening of 27 May 1993 as the longest in his life. Quarter past six was the moment he found the most exciting bird of his career. The twenty minutes were the time it took for two friends to run like hell to the spot where Mark was standing, on the shingle ridge that extends westwards from Cley Coastguards.

When they arrived the two friends could confirm that he had indeed just found Britain's first spring and Norfolk's first ever Desert Warbler. But for Mark what had converted those 1200 seconds of elation into a Jurassic period of hell was the fact that he had been a recent controversial witness to a couple of other rarities. Two was already looking a bit like carelessness; a third would have been disaster. Mercifully for Mark, *his* Desert Warbler stayed four days and eventually built a nest. Hundreds got to see it. As he himself wrote later, he didn't walk home that evening. He 'floated back to Cley'.

Another thing you should try to ensure for your first is that it doesn't ever become too easy to see. A second or a third over subsequent years is fine, but several million is a definite no-no. Probably the most degraded of all British firsts were the Collared Doves found by Michael Seago at Overstrand in north Norfolk on 3 July 1956. At the time it was such a hush-hush record that in the published account the birds' locations were only referred to as Site A or Site B. Little did they realise that this was just the vanguard of a massive invasion. By the time I first picked up binoculars the doves had ripped through Britain like a Panzer division and colonised us from Cornwall to Shetland. Now it's the tenth most-common bird in our gardens. Even so, it's testimony to the irreducible authority of a first that when Michael died in 1999 his discovery of the Collared Dove was repeatedly cited in his obituaries.

To acquire a truly immortal legend it is best to weave some lovely little anecdote into the story of your discovery of the bird. One of my favourites concerns Richard Richardson. Almost inevitably he was involved in the finding of several firsts. He had a part in the Collared Dove record at Overstrand, but he was also one of the main observers to identify Britain's first example of a small American wader called Semipalmated Sandpiper. It was on

Arnold's Marsh just off East Bank. (Of course! Where else could it have been?) In order to clinch the identification, Richard went out on to the mud looking for the bird's footprints, which could possibly have revealed the presence of narrow webbing between the toes, from which the bird takes its name. Unfortunately the goo was too soft to retain those semipalmations accurately, but I cherish that image of Richardson plouting about in the middle of Arnold's up to his knees in black sludge.

Richard's was a great first. But of all the birds found during my own lifetime, the one which seems most perfect, a first not just for Britain but for the entire Western Palearctic, was the Ancient Murrelet found on 27 May 1990.

Synthliboramphus antiquus was truly a first with everything. Not the least of its charms is that extraordinary scientific name. It breeds on island chains and coastlines across the Bering Sea, from northern Japan to the American state of Washington. Unlike, say the Pallas's Sandgrouse, it had no pre-existing claim on our imaginations because no one expected such a bird could turn up. As the murrelet flies it was half a world away from home. Who knows which route it took to the Bristol Channel, but each involved an unprecedented journey. It had never even been seen on the eastern seaboard of North America, let alone on this side of the Atlantic.

What it may have lacked in beauty, it more than made up for with sheer personality. Steel grey above and white below, it is something like a small, stubby, smartly dressed Puffin without the multicoloured bill. Its most striking feature is a pair of long 'bushy' white lines across the side of the crown which look like Michael Foot's eyebrows and which meet on the nape to give the bird its 'Ancient' tag.

It was definitely a beast with both a sense of location and of timing. It appeared for several weeks in three consecutive springs – 1990–1992 – and almost always on Lundy (it was once seen from a boat six miles out from the Devonshire islet). While thousands of birders managed to see it during that period, it never made itself too available. A showing of four minutes a day was a regular average. There were some unfortunates who made the effort more than once to reach Lundy and still didn't connect with it. Needless to say when its brief and wandering life was finally extinguished, probably somewhere out in the Atlantic, no other Ancient Murrelet has ever repeated its exploits. That bird was our one and only opportunity. All this helps compound its status as one of the top firsts of the century. Yet for me what distinguishes it most is the sheer chance and the extraordinary web of coincidence that lie behind its discovery. This involved two very fortunate (im)mortals – Richard Campey and Keith Mortimer.

Richard is well known in the birding world partly because many of us buy our optics from him. He's a director for the biggest binocular and telescope dealers in Britain. His other claim to fame was a lead role in a 1990s ITV programme called *Wild About the West* that ran for four series and about fifty half-hour slots on environmental issues in the south-west. It was a magazine-style show with three presenters. Items were co-delivered and the thread of narration bounced between them in a sequence of short alternating snippets that were always exchanged with now-over-to-you turns of the head and bursts of eye-contact. It was meant to seem spontaneous and natural. In fact, it looked tightly scripted and heavily choreographed. One could almost sense the control-freak producer breathing down their necks. It was like Esther Rantzen's *That's Life*, but on raised peat bogs and recycling garden waste. Yet it worked and had peak audiences of several million.

Richard, however, has my undying admiration for seeing through the shallowness of a career on the box and chucking it in for a life in commerce. What makes him even more admirable is that he was a TV natural. Boyish good looks and a razor-sharp wit – he was destined for great things. Who knows where he would have ended, but some in the business suggested he'd be perfect for the recent vacancy on *Songs of Praise*.

Now that would have been . . . interesting. An atheist ecologist with a penchant for rare birds and racy one-liners.

In the rarities stakes Richard has already enjoyed more success than any unbeliever really deserves, although he has hedged his bets by spending part of every spring and/or autumn of the last twenty-three years tramping around on Lundy. It is a clever tactic. Lundy, like Fair Isle or the Scillies, and several other offshore islands, is a hotspot for migrants. Birds, driven by strong winds and disruptive climatic conditions elsewhere in the world, are frequently pushed off their normal migration route and end up thousands of miles from home. As they approach Britain they frequently make landfall on the first available *terra firma*, and that's usually some pinprick off the mainland coast.

While Lundy has a reputation for rarities, you can spend a fortnight scouring the island and see nothing more interesting than its resident seabirds, one migrant Whinchat and half a dozen Willow Warblers. It's a gamble not every birder is prepared to take. But the flipside of this is obvious. When something rare does turn up you stand a strong chance of finding it yourself.

And that's the joy, in fact, the drug, to which Richard is slave. His triumphs include Little Bunting (about 650 British records), Alpine Swift (about 560 records), two Short-toed Larks and a Rose-coloured Starling (both about 500 records), two Subalpine Warblers (about 400 records), Black Kite (about 250 records and found on the same day as his Little Bunting), Baillon's Crake (about 75), Semipalmated Sandpiper (the thirty-fifth record) and Sardinian Warbler (the thirteenth record).

He had become so addicted to the island that for two years, 1978–80, he lived and worked there as acting warden for the island's managers, the Landmark Trust, from whom he drew a weekly wage of a fraction under fifty pence. This princely sum was supplemented with the manager's post at Lundy's only watering hole, the Marisco Tavern. It was a career combination that encompassed most of Richard's favourite activities. The pub job brought in an additional £39.56 after tax and as many free drinks as he could manage. During the more sober moments of each week, the acting warden also shot about fifty of Lundy's legions of rabbits, which he exchanged with Belgian trawlers for boxloads of fresh fish.

Richard was living like a king and it was exactly this enchanted career that Keith Mortimer, one of his best mates, inherited from him in 1980. Keith kept the post for twice as long, giving them a grand combined total on Lundy of six years.

By rights, you would have thought that Richard or Keith would have found the Ancient Murrelet during this six-year vigil, perhaps on one of those days when they were working the island alone, completely focused on rarities. And because their stints as warden were in different years you'd also imagine just one of them would have found it by himself – the sort of life-separating experience to get any pair of twins at each other's throat. But no. When it comes to rare birds, blind fate can sometimes touch us with a lanugo-like softness.

Paul Doherty, for instance, bumped into Europe's first ever Golden-winged Warbler as he walked to post a letter on the Lundsford Park Estate in New Hythe, Kent. When he found it he didn't even have his binoculars. On 7 February 1989 this gorgeous little New World bird should have been in high-altitude cloud-forest in Guatemala. Instead it was in the bushes by Tesco's. Two days after Paul found it there were 3000 birders in that supermarket car park.

The murrelet's discovery involved the same degree of pure and gentle fortune. Although the bird was on Lundy, neither Keith nor Richard were staying at the time. Nor were they hunting for rarities. Nor were they by themselves. Instead they had 265 other people with them on a Sunday outing in search of Puffins. It was an RSPB-organised Centenary Cruise and both of Lundy's ex-wardens had shared responsibility for this particular day trip.

It all passed off calmly as they shepherded part of the flock over to the west side of the island and a spot known as Jenny's Cove, where small numbers of Puffins breed. They enjoyed a perfectly pleasant half-hour pointing them out to the punters, as the charismatic seabirds came and went from the Lundy clifftops. Pleasant, that is, until the moment one client said to them, 'Is this another Puffin?' . . . and it was a murrelet.

As soon as Richard and Keith saw the pert little seabird they were instantly sure of just one thing – it was completely unlike any other bird they'd ever seen. That's when the heart really starts pounding and the first battle is to suppress the mounting delirium and keep the brain functioning. There are thirteen small auk species in the world. Just one of them occurs routinely in Europe, invariably in autumn, an Arctic bird called Little Auk. Very occasionally such birds appear in the wrong season or, potentially, with aberrant plumages. An absence of pigmentation can result in odd variations like partial or complete albinos.

As soon as Richard and Keith had eliminated the much more prosaic possibility that it was a partial albino Little Auk, the real agony began. Here was their moment of destiny. Yet as they struggled with the knotted conundrum of the murrelet's identity, they were surrounded by a crowd of birding beginners who wanted to share with them different sorts of uncertainty. Questions like, 'Is that a Shag on the rocks?' . . . 'Is a Shag the same as a Cormorant?' . . . 'Will we see any Shags today?' . . . 'Those are nice binoculars – how far can you see with them?'

The only question they were really bothered about was – 'What the . . . F%*& is this seabird just two-thirds the size of a Puffin?' The other twelve small auks in the world are all inhabitants of upper and middle latitudes in the Pacific. Richard and Keith had never been there and these sorts of birds never feature in a British field guide. Besides, no self-respecting birder would ever *dream* of carrying a field guide in the field. And on your local patch most of us would rather die than risk being seen looking through one. There is no more humiliating admission of inadequacy. It meant there was only one thing for it. Richard and Keith had to run like hell to get the field guide from the pub.

We're closing in now on the key couple of minutes that I particularly want to describe in the murrelet's discovery. In fact if the act of finding rare birds were ever treated in a field guide of its own, then the identification arrows would all be pointing at this pivotal and diagnostic moment.

It was the second the two of them stopped midway through the two-mile run to the Marisco Tavern and turned to one another, faces beaming in recognition of what was just then coming to pass. And there, amongst the heather, witnessed only by the smiling heavens above, these two young adult men, sound of mind and body, proceeded to punch the air, screaming and whooping in demented exultation. Periods of frenzied leaping were exchanged with episodes on the bare ground, rolling doggo or lying belly up in a cushion of heather, kicking blissfully at the ether. If ever a moment speaks for all birders in their hour of finding *their* great bird, then this is it.

Those heartsongs of praise, those moments of release, were quickly followed by the strangulating fear tht they wouldn't be able to nail the bird's identification and that someone else might sneak up in their short absence and steal the record . . . But we needn't worry.

By the time they were heading back from the pub to Jenny's Cove and returning to their colleague, John, who'd kept tabs on the bird and already suggested it might be a murrelet, Richard and Keith had narrowed it down to one of two species. The illustration in the book, *Seabirds*, a seminal tome covering all the marine species in the world by Peter Harrison, didn't show *Synthliboramphus antiquus* particularly well. During the first hours they weren't sure if they were dealing with Crested or Ancient Murrelet, although even this uncertainty was soon eliminated.

By the time they were steaming victoriously into Ilfracombe, Richard, Keith and the others who had seen it, had got hold of another seabird book that illustrated the Lundy bird to perfection. They were all in agreement which new species for Britain and the Western Palearctic they'd just found. Richard rushed up to the boat's tannoy system to announce the happy tidings to the world.

That very evening Steve Gantlett was on the phone to his good friends in Salthouse, Ron and Sue Johns, newly back for the second time from the Pallas's Sandgrouse on Shetland. Some strange character had just been on the phone, says Steve, telling him he'd been on Lundy and found a . . . But then you know the rest. It's history, ancient (murrelet) history.

It's finally time for the chapter to head briefly into outer space so that we can get a proper sense of perspective on all the four dimensions in which the affair unfolded. First, let's recap. Richard and Keith were, in fact, still are, best friends. That in itself is part of the miracle of the murrelet. They were both also fanatical Lundyites. It is probably their favourite place on earth to go birding. Both had wardened the island. Between them they had scoured Lundy's valleys and headlands almost daily for a combined total of 2200 days. Yet they had found the bird, not during these intensive years of Lundy bashing, but on a shared daytrip to show Puffins to beginners – the only day that year, in fact, when they were together on the island. Contemplate briefly how different it would all have been if one had found it . . . and the other had not.

Let's now bring the bird into this long equation. It had travelled to Britain, a minimum linear distance of 7000 miles, alone and across millions of square miles of open water. Then, on completely the wrong side of the planet, with huge stretches of European coastline on which to live out its solitary, disoriented years, it had chosen Lundy as a base of operations. On that sunny Sunday in May when it had first revealed its presence to the British birding community it should have been on its breeding grounds on some salt-fretted promontory on the Pribilofs or the Aleutians. Instead it was bobbing like a cork in the Bristol Channel.

Think of all the millions of small, chance possibilities and variations that could have so easily prevented these three separate lives from ever colliding in this fashion. Yet some strange and beautiful force, some weird karmic thrust had impelled them through the chaos to that flash of *satori*-like lucidity, that moment of intersection on 27 May 1990. It is this miraculous coincidence, this sense of a guiding hand, of someone looking down and touching us with the wand of destiny, that makes the rare bird such an awesome and blessed occasion for birders.

Reflecting on the divine symmetry involved in the murrelet's discovery, Richard once said, 'It almost, ALMOST makes you believe in God.' I'm just thinking how that might have gone down on *Songs of Praise*.

14

The Yanomami Hunters

1 Blyth's Reed Warbler, Acrocephalus dumetorum
St Agnes, Scilly, 14–16 October 1979

It's an almost predictable pattern. Non-birders hear stories like the finding of the Ancient Murrelet or other rare birds and they're instantly struck by what seems to them a central mystery of birding. Usually the confusion is expressed in questions like, 'But how can you tell if someone's making it up or not?' or 'What's to stop me simply *saying* I've just seen a Great Auk or a Lesser-spotted So-and-so, when I haven't?'

The answer is perfectly simple. There's absolutely nothing to stop someone lying about what they see. On the other hand, it's also devilishly complicated. Because if you do make it up, you risk losing almost everything it means to belong to the tribe. That paradox is at the very core of birding culture. And without it the oral traditions we hold so dear would virtually wither on the vine, since birders talk endlessly on the issues of honesty and its corollary, credibility.

But a presumption of honesty is undoubtedly the starting point for all birders. The fabric of information on which we rely depends in turn on collective observations and records from all our peers. To doubt them would leave us in chaos. When I write that there are about 4,400,000 pairs of Blackbird in Britain it is not just a statement of fact, it's an act of faith. We *have* to believe that when thousands of birders submit their own handful of records of *Turdus merula* – on which the final population statistics are based – they do so in all honesty. Each fragment of data, however trivial, bears the impress of a birder's credentials.

And the sum of all those records is our reputation. Every birder has one. A nebulous, shifting, collective judgement on our birding abilities, which acts as a type of rank, file and serial number within the tribe. Nothing is ever written down. Not unless you want to end up in a libel court. But that reputation is critical. It is the key adhesive that glues the whole community, in fact the whole process, together. It's the hallmark of authenticity for every bird we claim. So the first thing a birder asks on hearing of a rarity, such as the Ancient Murrelet, is not, 'Could he have made it up?' but 'Who's seen it?' The answer to this question automatically implies an answer to the previous query.

Fortunately, most of the time reputation never truly becomes an issue. Our records are quietly acknowledged and blandly accepted. Our birding is conducted in an atmosphere of blameless obscurity.

Yet if you aspire to a more elevated status, then you have to do something a little more interesting. This can take a variety of forms. You can take and publish a set of unique photographs, write a ground-breaking book or identification paper, set up a new society and worm your way on to a bird-related committee. But finding a rarity is the classic means of rising above your former anonymity. That sense of blessed fortune may be a key element in your personal pleasure at turning up rare birds, but your peers honour the discovery as something other than a stroke of good luck.

All birding, not just finding and identifying rarities, involves a relatively complex intellectual process. Birds are distinguishable by variations on a number of fairly constant themes. Take the wader family. Seventy-four species have occurred in Britain. On any autumn day in Norfolk you might expect to find about thirty of these. They're all separable by small differences in overall size, length and colour of the bill or the legs, the length of their wings, the presence and absence of white in the wing, or the size of that white in the wing, or by the sound that the bird makes. In order to make a correct judgement on any single bird's identity you have to hold all the identification criteria simultaneously in your mind and apply a process of elimination to them preferably while the bird is on show. It sounds taxing, but with practice bird recognition becomes instinctive and instantaneous even on the briefest of views.

And it brings its own particular kind of satisfaction. Non-birders readily appreciate the aesthetic appeal of birds when attempting to understand why others go birding. It's much easier to overlook the seductive pleasures that are inherent in the identification process. An example will clarify the point.

We're standing on the shingle bank at Cley staring out to sea on a salt-fresh, sun-washed day in April. Over the dark water a small huddle of birds is hurrying against the brisk north-easterly, about a third of a mile out. They're all waders. Gradually the flock emerges from the darkly shadowed water into a passing pool of sunshine. In that brief magnesium flare of light you recognise them – their large size, the long upturned bills, the vivid chestnut underparts – as Bar-tailed Godwits on their way to breeding grounds in Arctic Siberia. They and their wonderful migration out of Africa are classic symbols of spring. And part of the alchemy of that season is the godwit's sumptuous terracotta plumage now dazzling in the sunlight.

Yet tucked in amongst these nine godwits, partly obscured by them, is another wader, paler above but similarly brick-red below and altogether smaller and shorter-billed. Every few seconds it shows amongst the constant flicker of migratory wings and as they all dip periodically below the blue-black water and the white surge of mare's tails. Eventually you realise. The odd one out is a Knot and you picked it out from the others as it made its own Arctic-bound journey.

The ten birds are all similarly beautiful in that rich summer dress, but without the identification they'd have slipped past as a flock of brick-red birds and nothing more. What rounds the experience off as a process of discovery, what converts your sighting into a moment of interception in the waders' heroic biennial journey, is that commonplace act of recognition. And the whole encounter is tinged with the enchantment of knowing. It's what lured humanity out of Eden.

Separating a Knot from a Bar-tailed Godwit is a simple business, but even some daily garden-bird identifications involve millimetre-accurate judgements. The separation of some species can involve scrutiny of a single tract of feathers, such as the median coverts or the tertials, or the size of one set of feathers relative to another. A classic confusion pair is Willow Warbler and Chiffchaff. One of the key means of identifying them is the greater projection in Willow Warbler of the main flight feathers, the primaries, beyond the tertials. Usually you have to spot these 3–4 millimetres of wingtip as the bird flits amongst the treetops.

This intellectual challenge is the silent arrow in the birder's great sheaf of motivations. Most are driven to go on adding to the repertoire of micro-judgements between different birds until they hold thousands of these points of separation in their heads. There are British and American birders, specialists in the avifauna of South America, who can identify as many as 2000 species by their calls alone.

I suspect that these top birders are amongst the most acutely skilled interpreters of nature on the planet. They are the Yanomami hunters of post-industrial society. Many other types of naturalist are working with similarly forensic detail. Students of the Arachnidae, for instance, are examining the genitalia to tell one species of spider from another. Botanists are searching for the glabrous hairs on the underside of the sepals. But these forms of identification involve static subjects. The spider's bits are beneath the microscope slide. If you can't decide whether the hairs are glabrous and the hand-lens isn't helping, then pick the plant and take it home to your library. Or post it to an expert. But in 99 per cent of birding situations you're looking at a rapidly moving target in the field. Any minute now it could fly away. Sometimes they do. Occasionally in birding there are no second chances and at times identification feels like a type of performance.

It has a sense of theatre that rare birds only serve to intensify. Clearly, the stakes are far higher. The birds themselves are inherently unfamiliar. Judgements about size, shape and colour are that much more difficult, but correspondingly more critical. If you get it wrong you risk the possibility of ridicule, even if it's just self-ridicule. If you get it right, hundreds, possibly thousands of other birders will go to see it. And when that happens, your millimetre-accurate judgements have to stack up with all of them. It can actually be a blessing when the bird disappears never to be seen again.

Then there are all the other considerations. The discovery of the Ancient Murrelet probably triggered more visits to Lundy over the three years of its stay than any other single attraction. It had knock-on benefits for the economy of the entire island. When Paul Doherty found his Golden-winged Warbler outside Tesco's at New Hythe, it drew some of the largest crowds of birders ever seen in Britain. In the resulting carnival atmosphere the local Girl Guides threw up an impromptu hotdog stall and made a small fortune.

In the context of the tribe, finding a rarity is instant proof of ability. It's a rite of passage into true hunter status. To repeat it over and over is to be elevated even further. Non-birders frequently presume that a birder's rank is measured by the length of a list. Not so. Even top twitchers acknowledge that the number of species seen is secondary, if not immaterial, to your reputation. In fact to have seen a large number of species without any parallel credentials as a field observer invites its own kind of scorn. The high list is then seen as merely a triumph over time, distance and financial limitation. Reputation, by contrast, is something money can't buy.

I said that Richard Richardson met on equal terms with those who, by the cultural mores of the 1940s and 1950s, might otherwise have thought themselves his social betters. Richardson's exceptional, undisputed abilities in the field swept all that away. To see a person spot a juvenile Long-tailed Skua at a mile's range and instantly identify it, when you know you could never do it yourself, is to behold something as wonderful almost as the bird itself. And it demands respect.

That elevated status doesn't just come from finding rarities. In fact the exact reverse can be the case, as happened on the island of St Agnes in the Scillies in October 1979. The incident involved an extremely rare bird, a member of the genus *Acrocephalus*, called Blyth's Reed Warbler. The Acros, the standard birder's term for the group, are one of the most difficult in the Western Palearctic.

Four species, Marsh, Reed, Blyth's Reed and Paddyfield Warblers are known as 'unstreaked acros' and are separable only by small structural variations and marginal differences in the tone of brown or colour of legs and bill. While the first two are widespread in Europe, only the Reed Warbler is a common British bird. Blyth's Reed and Paddyfield, by contrast, are both Sibes – vagrants from the Far East.

Part of the difficulty of separation is their skulking behaviour. For much of the time they remain in dense cover. Their movements are often traceable only by a constantly repeated metallic contact call. Frequently you get a composite image of the bird, pieced together from various fragmentary views. A wing for a few seconds, then the tail when it emerges twenty minutes later. After an hour's wait the bill and head may be seen clearly for the first time. In three hours of standing and watching, the bird could have been in view for a couple of minutes, never all at once.

In 1979 Blyth's Reed Warbler had been recorded just eleven times. Only one of those records was of a live bird. Most of the others had been shot in the early 1900s – a period before the development of high-quality optics, when birders usually needed the actual skin to make the kinds of detailed assessments necessary for identification. But it tells you a great deal about the problems of separating *Acrocephalus* warblers in autumn plumage. Even in the hand not all of them are identifiable.

This particular one, however, had been found on private land on St Agnes and while there were 300 birders hoping to see it, we were only to be allowed on to the site in batches – a few at a time for ten to fifteen minutes each. The rota was policed by a self-selected band of birding authority figures, but it ran perfectly smoothly and seeing the Blyth's Reed in relays like this only heightened the tension. Each of us had to wait patiently for his turn, sometimes queuing for hours, until eventually it was mine.

I was guided into a tiny fallow bulb field surrounded by tall pittosporum hedges. It was a sunny day and the bird was uncharacteristically obliging. After a few minutes this mythically rare Sibe popped into view, then dropped down into a weedbed just a few feet from where we stood. Repeatedly it would emerge from the greenery with a fat caterpillar, which it carried into the hedge to dismember and eat.

It was a triumphant moment and so captivating that I went to the back of the queue several times so that most of the day was absorbed with the one individual bird. Over successive periods I got to see most of its features in great detail – the long dagger-like bill with its evenly straw-coloured lower mandible, its bright straw legs and yellowish feet, the warm buff undertail coverts as it manoeuvred to thrash those caterpillars into extinction. On other occasions, as it plunged down amongst the weeds, you could see the warm, almost gingery tone to the mid-brown upperparts. And there were the evenly spaced primaries extending to the tips of the slightly paler and warmer uppertail coverts.

It was a thoroughly satisfying experience of the bird and I saw all the features wonderfully well. The only trouble was they weren't the features of a Blyth's Reed Warbler. They were the classic identikit parts of a young Marsh Warbler. The legs and feet should have been a dead give-away. On

Blyth's Reed they're dull grey. Our bird had toes the colour of ripening bananas.

But most of us weren't worried about these kinds of detail. We were told there was a Blyth's Reed Warbler on St Agnes. We queued all day to see a Blyth's Reed Warbler. When our allotted moment came why should we have wanted it to be a Marsh Warbler? We'd seen a Marsh Warbler the previous week on one of the other islands. Much better that it be something rare. Better still a rare Sibe. Best of all a rare Sibe unstreaked Acro – *Acrocephalus dumetorum*. We weren't Yanomami hunters, we were Pavlov's dogs. We'd been led towards a single knee-jerk response and most of us made it. It amounted almost to a mass hallucination. But there was at least one person who hadn't seen it that way.

As well as a floppy sunhat that might have been bought off one of the Flowerpot Men, Pete Grant always wore a pair of large black square-rimmed glasses that made him look a bit like a young Eric Morecambe. Maybe it was those huge specs that allowed Peter to keep a sense of detachment, even a sense of humour, about himself and the world.

Certainly they helped to make him into a field observer with perhaps the highest reputation of any British birder in the second half of the twentieth century. Certainly no one had higher. Grant was a star. By the age of twenty-eight he had already been invited on to the *British Birds* Rarities Committee, which had been in existence since 1958 to assess all records of rare birds in the country. Within five years he was its chair, reflecting his national and, increasingly, international reputation. By the end he was probably one of the best field observers in the world. Sadly, Pete was destined to fulfil another part of a common pattern amongst Britain's top fieldmen. He died young. And like Richard Richardson he died young from inoperable cancer. Grant was just forty-six.

Yet in that short life his influence was huge. Perhaps partly for sentimental reasons – since it was published nine years after his death – his name appears prominently on the new *Collins Bird Guide*. That alone was a fine epitaph. Many people consider it the finest bird field guide produced for our region, even any region.

But Pete's impact was strongly felt through a string of seminal papers on the identification of problematic birds. He was almost inevitably drawn to particularly difficult groups of birds where forensic detail is of paramount importance. This included the 'Acros' and another brain-twisting genus of warblers called *Hippolais*; 'Hippos' for short.

Gulls were his major speciality. No coincidence perhaps that they are probably the most difficult of all bird families in the entire northern hemisphere. Grant's meticulously observant methods were finally expressed in what amounted to the birder's equivalent of a political pamphlet. It was called the 'New Approach' and it was a detailed restatement of the forensic methods. Feather by feather, tract by tract, was Grant's cautious and methodical style. It included by inference a declaration of war on the idea of jizz. Identifying birds by an almost artistic, intuitive grasp of the bird's indefinable essence was presumably anathema to a personality which, in everyday life, expressed itself as a sales rep for Johnson's Wax.

An agent for household cleaning products and a Yanomami hunter – I suppose it's a strange combination, but that's how I see Pete Grant, and it speaks volumes about the nature of modern British birding. On 15 October 1979 on St Agnes, the top man for Johnson's Wax resisted the notion that, because he'd been *told* it was a rare bird, therefore it was one. Pete liked to play a little mind game in which he blotted out what everyone else was saying and made up his own mind. It sounds simple. But 300 of us could testify how difficult it is in practice. Unlike us, Grant looked at the Blyth's Reed and saw those yellow feet and concluded that it was probably wasn't one. The following day the bird was caught in a net and its biometrics were critically examined in the hand. Sure enough it was a Marsh Warbler. In such rare moments of independent judgement, and in the face of almost unanimously opposed opinion, are the reputations of great birders born.

15

String

1 (wooden) adult male Black Lark, Melanocorypha yeltoniensis
Donna Nook, Lincolnshire, 19 January 1991

Though belching is entirely socially acceptable, there is
the strongest possible taboo against breaking wind; it is
among the deadliest of all social sins. Most of the Arabs
have done so at one time or another during their lives,
but it is so memorable an event that by it other more
momentous happenings are dated; it remains evergreen
in the memories. When asked for the date of a murder
or a family disaster a man may muse and then reply, 'I
don't know; I think it was the year that Jassim farted.'

Gavin Maxwell, *A Reed Shaken by the Wind*

There's only one crime that causes the same kind of stink and
which is as arbitrary and categorical amongst birders. It's called
stringing. As verb, noun and adjective, string describes the act of
making up birds. String is a sin that strikes at the very heart of
birding. We don't tolerate it. We seldom forgive it. Once labelled,
a person often goes to their grave with the mark, as if it were
indelibly tattooed in capitals across their forehead – STRINGER.

String is integrally linked to the notion of a birder's reputation.
Both are driven by a similar motivation – a wish to excel and be
noticed – but one is the flipside of the other. And if reputation
is the adhesive that glues the birding community together, string

is the solvent that sets it unravelling. A large part of a person's concern for his or her reputation is their fear of the slur of string. Simply to be free of such a taint is as much reputation as many birders ever seek.

Defining string precisely is difficult because birders place different interpretations on the label. The first thing we can do, however, is distinguish it from genuine error, something which all birders commit. Even top birders like Pete Grant make mistakes. In fact their momentary lapses are stored and cherished with the relish that we recall their flashes of brilliance. They confirm that our heroes are only human. During our own moments of confusion in the field, they soothe troubled egos by reminding us that you can have a top reputation but still balls things up now and then.

It must be said that some birders even lump this form of genuine error into the category of string, but I have to reject this. A misidentification is merely a technical failure, pure and simple, without any form of ulterior intention. And here we get at a centrally defining characteristic of string. In doing it the perpetrator has a hidden purpose and motive, usually to claim the renown that attaches to finding rarities. We can say categorically, therefore, that no one would ever be accused of string for misidentifying a rare bird as a common species.

String by contrast involves error *plus* motive *plus* – even more crucially – deception. Clearly, to claim a bird you have never seen is to deceive, at some level, your fellow birders. And the heinous character of the crime is in direct proportion to the extent you set out deliberately to mislead others. It amounts to outright cheating and is the form of string no birder would dispute.

But much more interesting, much more difficult to ascertain, is the extent to which string is the act of deceiving oneself. On this question birders divide again into two camps. Some infamous stringers, with long lists of dubious records to their names, are exonerated by a section of their peers on the plea that while the birds are clearly bogus, the persons claiming them honestly and genuinely believe they have seen what they allege they have seen. Thus they cannot be guilty, in Sartrean terms, of some form of ornithological bad faith, and are, therefore, not guilty of string.

I sense this is now getting too complicated. So let's have an example to clear things up a little.

A person is looking off Titchwell in north Norfolk and catches a glimpse of a flying bird that's common in north Norfolk and on most coastlines around Britain, a Sandwich Tern. He sees the individual but only as it's flying away, so the observer omits to note the clear yellow tip to its all-black bill. Sandwich Tern has a counterpart species called Gull-billed Tern, which is similar in size and colour but its beak is thicker, shorter and entirely black. The Sandwich Tern has a bill that's a maximum of 2.4 centimetres longer; at their closest, however, the difference is just 11 millimetres. The difference in bill depth, meanwhile, is just 5–10 millimetres. The other crucial difference between the two is that while Sandwich Terns breed in their thousands just along the coast on Scolt Head island, Gull-billed Tern is extremely rare. There have only been 260 records ever in Britain.

Our observer, having failed to note the diagnostic yellow tip to the tern's bill, lets his imagination supply the missing details. Eventually he comes to conclude it *was* the much rarer of the two birds. By the time he commits anything to paper he gives himself even more benefit of the doubt, and is convinced that the bill wasn't just all black, it was also short and stubby.

By the time he speaks to the first birder to come along after he's seen it, he's now recalling even more detail: the more extensive black cap, the elegant flight and the proportionately broader wings. While the white rump he never actually saw has become an unmistakable grey and more or less concolorous with the back. Finally, at the moment our stringer writes the record up to submit it to the BBRC, the *British Birds* Rarities Committee, it is a description of a Gull-billed Tern in perfect detail, which is not surprising because much of it is copied word for word from the field guide.

I suspect that this is how an episode of string would unfold and, for me, it involves both deception of others and, at some more complex level, deception of oneself. The stringer both believes in his string *and* knows he's done it simultaneously. That's what makes him such a fascinating creature.

It was partly in an attempt to regularise and protect the integrity of ornithological records and to screen out this type of bogus claim that the birding establishment set up the BBRC in 1958. The committee used the journal *British Birds* as a vehicle both for soliciting proper descriptions of particularly unusual species, which have become known as BB rarities, and publishing those records that had been accepted. Initially there was a team of ten, the famous 'ten rare men', comprising some of the top field observers of the time. Today this has expanded to sixteen members, including an archivist, a museum consultant and two honorary statisticians. All are male and in its forty-three years there has never been a single female representative.

When it was first set up the committee examined just 200 records per year. Today this has risen to 1200–1500 birds, which are almost all described in minute and copious detail. For members it is a time-consuming and onerous bureaucratic duty discharged without any kind of financial return. Yet the huge honour it entails ensures that there's a steady stream of willing candidates and some stalwarts serve for as long as ten years.

The committee members are credited with an uncanny sixth sense about a dubious record. Pete Grant reckoned in his day that just 2 per cent of falsely identified birds are accepted (other BBRC members thought this might be an underestimate). On the other hand Grant thought 5 per cent of genuine rarities were wrongly rejected. Many of these unaccepted birds are probably discounted on the technical inadequacy of the documentation, rather than any disbelief in the observer.

The collective rigour applied to the records is high and getting higher. In some notable cases supporting photographs or video footage are sent away for professional examination in order to eliminate the possibility of fraud. Members tacitly ring around to check on an observer's reputation and his 'track record' in rarities. For some notorious individuals a kind of informal data bank builds up on their exploits and their claimed birds are singled out for the third degree.

Even so, some of the stunts pulled by birding hopefuls almost beggar belief. One took the trouble to support his claim with a good photograph of the bird in question, an extreme rarity that would have been a first for Britain. Despite this corroborative evidence it was still, alas, a tad difficult to accept the record because you could see the blurred outline of the wires which were trapping the bird inside its cage.

Another stringer submitted a description of a rare bird that they claimed to have found near a bird observatory on the English south coast. The account was extremely detailed and accurate, which wasn't surprising because it had been copied verbatim from the observatory's logbook, where there was a written report of the same species, this bird the genuine article, caught and ringed two years previously. The account was identical to the log entry even down to the number of the ring clamped on the bird's leg, which bears a unique combination of figures so that if it were ever recaught the bird's movements could be monitored.

You'll notice I haven't given exact details in either of these cases. Although every birder is familiar with stories about string, it is a subject more than any other aspect of birding that's confined to the oral tradition. To be cast as a stringer is to lose your ornithological soul and endure an eternity of behind-the-hand whispers, but the perpetrators are seldom, if ever, directly confronted with their sins. Nothing has ever been written down and I wouldn't wish to break ranks now.

So for the purposes of exploring a subject that's socially, even legally, delicate, but absolutely central to birding culture, I've taken the precautionary step of a little string of my own. I've invented a birder whose career involves a distillation of many of the kinds of string of which birders are aware. He is my invention, but his exploits are not. The birds he claims to have found are, in a sense, double figments of the imagination, his and mine. But birds like them have been 'found' or claimed in the way I describe. He is, in short, completely fabricated but true in parts.

He is none other than Robert Barry Shutbill. Bob Shutbill – BB or, at one time, even 'Shrike' to his friends (because of the initials RBS: Red-backed Shrike), is, in fact, a damn good birder. And this instantly touches on one of the deeper mysteries of the stringer. They can be at once highly talented but still fatally flawed. Bob's flaws didn't show up initially and even today some of his mates still stand by him, putting his excesses down to occasional lapses of concentration or fits of over-imagination. Most also maintain that when Bob's in the field with them, he's a model of ability and caution.

For several years he was even seriously considered as a member of the *British Birds* Rarities Committee. In many ways it was that possible appointment which triggered the first major assault on his credibility. A story did the rounds on the grapevine that if Bob were invited to join the BBRC, then several other members were going to resign in protest. Other birders said that they would immediately cease to submit records because Bob's inclusion would call the committee's integrity into serious question. At the time the standard joke was that Shutbill's appointment would give a whole new meaning to a BB rarity.

I suspect that one of the main problems is that he's Shutbill by name, but not by nature. In most of the things he did he liked to make an impact. The desire for publicity is a recurrent characteristic amongst many stringers and I suspect that it is a root cause of the whole business. Although in the case of Bob's most famous exploit *why* exactly he did it remains, in the final analysis, largely inexplicable. No one has ever dared confront him outright, so to this day it's a mystery.

When I did ask close friends what had moved him to do it, their answers were deeply conflicting. Some argued it was out of contempt for fellow birders, others said that he cared desperately what other birders thought of him and simply wanted to belong and enjoy regard from those he himself admired. Curiously it was the contradictions in the answers that meshed most closely with my own clearest memory of Bob.

On that occasion we met him at Nancy's. The place was nearly full, which meant that in a space thirteen by thirteen feet, many of the sixteen seats around five tables were occupied. Intimate conversation was impossible, but the four of us were seated in a block and we were involved in a private discussion. As we continued, we became aware of a solitary figure on the adjacent table listening in to our talk as if he were directly included in what we were saying.

It was a weird moment. We didn't really know Bob except by reputation. But his manner suggested a curious tension, as if he wanted to be engaged and disengaged at the same time. While he was smiling and nodding he was also lolling casually back on his chair's back legs, his whole body pointed away towards the dining room's open door. Now and then we smiled or glanced in his direction perhaps to legitimise his involvement in our conversation, but it was all very awkward. I remember it was a relief when Nancy came through with the meal and we could get our heads down and avoid eye-contact. But most of the time he wasn't even looking at us, simply rocking back and forth, face lit by a half-smile, musing privately on the discussion or sharing some secret reflection with himself.

By that date there were already several secrets to which Bob alone had the answers. They centred on a number of exciting birds that he claimed to have found and seen, but which few others had managed to observe. Bob's a bright fellow and after getting a first in his MSc from a top Scottish university he had various jobs as a middle-ranking civil servant in the MOD and, latterly, at the Ministry of Agriculture. Initially he spent a lot of time at naval bases around northern Scotland, which gave him opportunities for birding in remote and underwatched parts of the country. It produced a sequence of very good rarities in just a couple of years, including a Ross's Gull, a Terek Sandpiper, a Paddyfield Warbler and, most notable of all, a white-morph Gyr Falcon, one of the most spectacular birds of prey to appear in these islands.

None of these rarities is particularly unexpected in northern Scotland and all were, in due course, accepted by the BBRC. Questions only started to be raised quietly when some bright spark noted that eight of his ten birds were single-observer records. That was rather odd because most rarities in Britain are seen by at least one other person. To put it in context, a top birder with a stainless reputation, Keith Vinicombe, has written that of the 41 rarities he's found 98 per cent have been seen by others. Equally illuminating, Chris Heard, one of the few birders with a reputation to rival Pete Grant's, has only three single-observer records from the extraordinary total of seventy-five rarities he's found. That no one had seen *any* of Bob Shutbill's birds, except for a juvenile Common Rosefinch and a Short-toed Lark – the least notable of his ten – despite the fact that he'd put the news out on all of them, was a niggling anomaly.

Amongst a group of Scottish birders vague curiosity hardened into fully fledged suspicion after a series of even more bizarre records by BB, the most notorious of which was a claim of seven Broad-billed Sandpipers together at a small wetland near Aberdeen. This wader is an inhabitant of high Arctic tundra, breeding no closer to Britain than central southern Scandinavia. It passes through Britain in very small numbers during the spring, with even smaller figures occurring during the reverse journey in the autumn. Bob's birds weren't only in autumn, there were more than twice as many as the previous largest party of Broad-bills ever seen in Britain. No one knew quite what to make of it. As far as I'm aware, when Bob submitted the record it was quietly shelved by the BBRC pending further evidence of his developing career as a 'rarity' finder.

That wasn't long in coming. A new job with MAFF involved a series of postings in Shropshire and later near the Nottinghamshire/Lincolnshire border. During the first period he took to seawatching off a previously overlooked promontory off Anglesey. Watching birds migrating just offshore has to be one of the most fulfilling forms of birding and some become so addicted to this one activity that they travel the world in search of new seawatching opportunities.

I can easily see why they become hooked. You sit with your scope fixed on a section of sea. And since pelagic bird migration is at its best in the roughest conditions, you're usually watching a wild scene of powerful gales and violent water. After several hours of intense watching your optics seem to lure you into that inhuman waterscape. And it's not just the background drama which gives seawatching its deep sense of theatre. The birds tend to slide through the white-crested breakers in a constant looping rhythm and you're usually filled with anticipation about what's going to loom into vision next. At the same time, there's a parallel sense of anxiety because seawatching is truly a one-shot deal. If you don't nail the bird's identity in those few minutes, and sometimes only seconds, that it's passing by, you're lost.

Seawatching has to be one of the ultimate tests of field skills but, ironically, it's also a stringer's paradise. No one can really challenge your records unless they're present when the bird's passing and they can see it for themselves. The only thing they can rely on to assess the observer's veracity is their overall reputation – there it is again – and the rough statistical probability of the claimed sightings. In Bob's case the stats went right out the window. Not only was it the huge numbers of relatively uncommon shearwaters, skuas and petrels he was seeing, it was also the really rare seabirds, some of which had been recorded on only a handful of occasions. Most bizarre was his claim to have seen Britain's and Europe's second Ancient Murrelet just after Richard and Keith's bird on Lundy.

By this time Bob had stopped submitting records to the BBRC because of the negative rumblings that surrounded his birds, but the word went round on the grapevine about what he was seeing off Anglesey and people started to try to join in the fun. The trouble was no one ever got to see anything like the numbers or the range of seabirds he was claiming and for his growing band of detractors it was a final nail in the coffin.

But there were those who were more incensed by another of Bob's foibles. He was also at one time a keen twitcher with a British list well in excess of 450. Unfortunately Bob's methods as a lister were also a subject for debate. However, in this instance it wasn't the bird's existence which was in question, because in twitching you're chasing other people's rarities. No, the birds were genuine all right, it was Bob's claim to have seen them which was in dispute.

Initial suspicions surfaced when a friend happened to catch a glimpse of Bob's computer screen while he was working on his list some time in the late 1980s. On page seven, the words BROWN THRASHER virtually leapt out of the screen at him. As you know, there's only been one Brown Thrasher in Britain, a bird at Durlston Head in Dorset, where it stayed from 18 November 1966 until 5 February 1967. Bob could have seen the thing during that period as he maintained. The problem was that as far as anyone knew Bob didn't pick up a pair of bins until 1967, when he was eight years old. The thrasher would have to have been one of the first birds he ever clapped eyes on. And that was his story. Apparently his parents had taken him there on a family outing and he just happened to have found it by chance. He said it was only years later when he realised that the weird brown bird he'd seen that afternoon must have been the thrasher. The pieces didn't add up, but no one could really pin him down.

The first time that happened was over the Chimney Swift. The bird appeared near Porthgwarra in Cornwall in October 1982. It was seen by hundreds of people and, remarkably, was joined by a second bird for three of its seven-day stay. Hardly anyone saw anything controversial in Bob's claim to have travelled down midweek to have seen this rare American species. Hardly anyone, that is, except the mate who happened to ring him up at work that day and was told by a colleague that Bob had just that second popped out the office and would be back in a moment. His friend thought nothing of it, until confronted with BB's passing remark the following night that he'd had really great views of the swift and was his friend going to go for it?

Naturally, this set tongues wagging and the friend, more in hope of discovering the work colleague had been confused over Bob's whereabouts, rather than out of a desire to nail the lie, rang round in the south-west to find out if anyone had actually seen Bob Shutbill in Cornwall on the day in question. But the enquiry drew a blank.

Next time, unfortunately, there was no room for doubt. It involved a Booted Warbler that turned up for a couple of days the following September at Spurn Head. By now a rota of friends had taken to ringing Bob at work, just in case he claimed any other mysterious twitching trips. And on that Monday, the 24th, they caught him red-handed.

Not only did two friends ring up and get put on hold by a secretary, one of them actually heard Bob speak before they quietly put the phone down as if to suggest it had been a wrong number. When Bob then claimed to have been for that Booted Warbler there was no way out. And what really left him up shit creek was the fact that on being questioned over the warbler, he said he'd seen it at the spot it had been found on the Sunday. The trouble was, by the Monday the bird had actually moved half a mile up the road and was only relocated at a new site in the afternoon. Bob was caught by a double whammy. He couldn't have been at Spurn because he was clearly in his office. And if he had been at Spurn he'd have known that the bird was no longer at the spot where he claimed to have seen it.

Who knows? Perhaps it was a desire to throw himself a lifeline out of the deepening mire, but Bob's next exploit looked like the action of a desperate man. Yet perhaps you can see the kind of twisted logic that might have motivated him. If only he could produce a photograph or a co-observer or some kind of corroborative evidence to confirm what he'd seen, then maybe he could prove that his detractors had been wrong about him all along. In the event it was his own camera that did the trick.

It was 19 January 1991. An anti-cyclone had been fixed over central Europe for weeks, pushing a north-easterly airstream straight from the frozen continent into much of eastern Britain. In my own notebook, each outing around this date had been logged with the prefatory words – 'extremely cold'. It was also freezing on the day that Bob Shutbill went out to check the fields and hedges around Donna Nook, a small spur jutting out into the Humber estuary just to the east of Cleethorpes on the northern Lincolnshire coast, almost immediately opposite Spurn Head. Bob had taken to watching the site regularly after he moved to Newark close to the Notts/Lincs border, pointing out that it was underwatched and the kind of place you could find your own rarities without stumbling over too many other birders.

Until that winter of 1991 there had been no BB claims to give anyone cause for alarm, but all that ended on the Saturday evening when he rang his friend Dave, and announced, 'I've really hit the jackpot this time!' That was Bob's way of breaking his fantastic story. As he then explained, he was checking a series of ploughed fields close to a thick hedge in the late afternoon, when a strange black-and-white bird with a yellow-horn bill suddenly appeared before him. On being disturbed the creature flew around revealing solidly black wings and giving a short wagtail-like call before plumping back down exactly where he'd first seen it. Without further ado Bob stuck out a camera with a 400 mm lens and fired off a whole roll of film.

Few species that are boldly black-and-white are hard to identify. What was more difficult was taking in the magnitude of his achievement. The bird was a male Black Lark, one of the most sought-after, dreamed-about firsts for Britain that any birder could imagine. And this time he had confirmatory evidence.

A male *Melanocorypha yeltoniensis* is not too dissimilar in shape to our common-or-garden Skylark, but the Black Lark is huge – in fact the biggest lark in the region – with a wingspan about the length of a Mistle Thrush's. In summer most of its body is a deep rich black, although with the autumn moult this becomes overlain by long buff or off-white tips to the crown, mantle and breast feathers. The overall effect is a complex pattern of crescentic barring from the base of its bill to the base of the tail and on the whole of the chest and flanks.

Normally it occurs no closer to Britain than the areas of Central Asian steppe to the east of the southern stretch of the Volga. From about Volgograd its distribution extends eastwards across Kazakhstan and western Siberia in a relatively narrow belt more or less centred on a latitudinal line of fifty degrees north. The minimum journey necessary for a British birder to encounter a Black Lark is about 3000 miles. In every one of these previous meetings it had been the birders who had had to do all the travelling. And until the 1990s getting into the bird's range in Soviet Siberia had never been easy.

However, there was one further aspect to the appeal of a Black Lark, which had to do with a number of previous claims of the bird in the early twentieth century. Black Lark had actually appeared on the British list from 1907 until 1962. This was based on claims of four birds supposedly shot and stuffed between 29 January and 18 February 1907 in the vicinity of Hastings in Sussex. The extraordinary record was then followed by two more also shot near Hastings in January 1915.

While there was no disputing that the birds were Black Larks, they were eventually dismissed as genuine vagrants with the exposure of a larger scandal that became known as the Hastings Rarities. These were 595 records of rarities that were all claimed from one small area of East Sussex between 1892 and 1930. It was such an unprecedented number of rarities that the birding establishment had always been highly suspicious. It was finally investigated by a small team in the 1950s and the fruits of their study was published in 1962 in a long paper filling an entire edition of *British Birds*.

Most people concluded that rare birds were being killed in the Middle East and elsewhere and shipped back to Britain on ice, where they were being sold as genuine British vagrants. For some bright spark it was a brilliant wheeze for making money out of gullible collectors. For Britain's birding community it was an outrageous scandal equivalent to the furore over Piltdown Man. One of the consequences was the ditching of the 595 Hastings birds. So, after a fifty-five-year holiday on the British list, the Black Larks were turfed out like a group of undesirable aliens. The Hastings Rarities proved that there was nothing new about modern stringing. But the intriguing possibility raised by Bob's Donna Nook bird, whose dates almost exactly coincided with the earlier records, was that the Hastings birds were genuine all along.

Whatever the truth of this little historical conundrum, it was certainly the case that on a scale of one to ten, Black Lark scored a comfortable eleven with most modern British twitchers. And that was Bob's apparently indisputable triumph. He was determined to enjoy its multifarious consequences and his 'I've-hit-the-jackpot' call to his friend Dave was the preliminary hairline crack in an eventual dam-burst of repercussions.

Within hours of the initial message, birders all over the country were making preparations to act upon the news. With a rarity like a Black Lark, the usual checks on behaviour – the obligations to work, to family or friends and the constraints of time or distance – all went instantly in abeyance. To be at Donna Nook as the sun came up the next day, where the bird was last seen, was paramount.

However, in the web of telephone calls that interlaced the country that night, there was an irregular note sounding amongst the exchanges on distance, locations, timings, pick-up points, directions. That note concerned Bob's previous backlog of unconfirmed rarities. Over the years this had had its own consequences. It now gave an uncertain edge to the expectant atmosphere that is so much a part of the pleasure of twitching. It meant that some birders, on hearing about his Black Lark, didn't even bother to go. It meant that some drove overnight, partly motivated by a desire to show solidarity with a friend. It meant that some went without any expectation of seeing a Black Lark, but didn't dare not go – just in case. Then there were others, like the carload from Luton whose vehicle spared them the agony of a fruitless search the following morning, when the engine caught fire on the motorway.

The anticlimax which the Luton carload missed that day was building steadily from dawn onwards. It was freezing cold, yet about 200 birders had arrived at Donna Nook. Bob himself soon appeared to lead the way, explaining in detail what the lark had done and also to bask in the triumph. But to some people his manner already seemed 'a bit strange'. Most of the group waited, as is customary, where the bird was last seen – near the ploughed fields in which Bob had found it. It struck some as a little odd that within a very short time Bob gave up waiting and drove away at high speed. He then proceeded to drive up and down the lanes stopping intermittently, presumably to scan the fields. People could see him way across the open ploughland, but it was curious the way he kept stopping and starting, never really giving himself time to search any area properly.

At about eleven o'clock, Bob steamed back to the point where most were waiting and by the time he reached the general assembly any bubble of expectation had burst and they were breaking up to leave. Those who had been a little puzzled by Bob's erratic behaviour were completely nonplussed by his comment when he stopped to talk to another group of birders he knew – a carful who had come from Cornwall and were now also departing. As they turned to leave, Bob was heard to say, 'If you're going to go out, you might as well go with a bang.'

By Monday lunchtime the Black Lark – the biggest twitch in Britain that winter – was passing without so much as a whimper. No one had seen it and few now bothered to look. Dave, his friend who had received Bob's first jubilant phone call, went back to Donna Nook several days later. Visiting the spot where a rare bird has been seen by large numbers, one often finds where the grass and vegetation have been trampled as the crowds of twitchers manoeuvre and jockey for a better view. When the bird is still there these flattened patches are useful tell-tale markers, indicating to subsequent birders where to wait and watch. But if the bird has gone, the old traces have a strange, rather tantalising atmosphere like the rumpled bedclothes from someone else's passion. At Donna Nook the trail was stone cold and within twenty minutes he felt he was wasting his time.

All that remained for Britain's birders was to wait for Bob's slides and to see what they had missed. From their point of view the photographic results couldn't have been worse. Although they were not frame-filling shots they were sufficiently good to show the bird's big straw-coloured bill. There were the zigzag black-and-white lines all over its head and back. There was the neatly scalloped effect on the breast and flanks. There, in short, was a winter adult male Black Lark in all its glory. And at exactly the spot where a few days before they had stood and watched themselves.

The effect was almost immediate. For many of those who had seen them and even amongst those who hadn't, the slides cast a sorry light on their weaseling doubts about Bob. They even put to shame all their snide remarks about his other rarities. He must have seen them after all. If he could find a Black Lark, he could easily have seen a white morph Gyr Falcon or even a flock of seven Broad-billed Sands. Bob's reputation was on its way to rehabilitation, as his friends always hoped.

Yet amongst the drift of discussions arose a mistier, more subtle set of impressions centred on the nature of the slides. Some of those who had seen them were impressed by the sharply depicted black-and-white bird featured in every one. But they also spotted several strange anomalies. Bob said he'd first seen it in the late afternoon and taken his shots with a 400 millimetre lens, yet the pictures showed that the light had been excellent for photography. How come in two successive shots the bird itself had appeared not to move, but the photographer's angle had? Hadn't he said he'd taken the photos from the car? Could it be that such a bird would allow this much movement around it? It almost looked as if it were part of a professional shoot with a . . . the words lingered in the air, then finally slipped out – with a *model*!

Once the penny dropped, nobody could look at the slides without seeing the bird's monumental inertia. And it was now undoubtedly leading to scandal. It also pointed to a level of premeditation that was deeply troubling. It meant that someone must have taken enormous pains to shape and paint a Black Lark. (In fact everyone was really impressed by the thing's lifelike qualities!) It meant that at some point at Donna Nook a dog-walker or a jogger could easily have seen a figure taking photographs on that freezing cold winter's day, adjusting his subject's position, then taking another. It meant that when he rang to announce, 'I've really hit the jackpot this time' . . . but, you can guess by now.

Most disturbing of all were the implications for that Sunday morning, when he appeared at the site, explaining to everybody what the bird had done and where to stand. I wasn't there, so I can only guess at the questions. But they would have been relentless, which is in the nature of birding. 'Where did you first find it?' 'Was it shy?' 'Did it call at all?' 'How far away were you when . . . ?' 'How many photos did you get?' 'What does it look like in flight?' 'Was it a full male?' 'What was it doing when you last saw it?' 'Did it fly off?' All those things to remember and keep them all straight.

There were now also strange retrospective glimpses – 'If you're going to go out, you might as well go with a bang' – that seemed to invite further speculation. Did he really think he could carry it off? What was he trying to do? If he could, would he really have submitted the record to try to get it accepted? And who was he ultimately cheating, the others or himself? In the end, all the questions I've asked myself over the years boil down to just two simple alternatives, a sort of final flip of the coin. How should we look at the story of Bob Shutbill's Black Lark – as a comedy, or was it really a tragedy?

When a set of slides finally ended up in Edinburgh several weeks later, a group of birders blew them up on a huge screen and all came to the same independent conclusion. They knew Bob well. He had been at university with some of them. On that January night they had actually gone over to Lincolnshire to show solidarity with a friend, but they couldn't now. As one of them later admitted, 'I felt it was part of my reputation on the line.' When Bob finally arrived himself to go birding, the subject had to surface. He was asked whether he was going to submit the record to the *British Birds* Rarities Committee. When Bob said that he was, it was suggested that he should think very carefully about it because he'd have to submit the slides. 'And if I were on the rarities committee,' a friend added, 'I'd have a lot of trouble thinking it wasn't a model.' For once Bob seemed lost for words and his face remained expressionless.

Since that January in 1991 I've never seen Bob birding in Britain, and he hasn't publicly claimed another rarity. There was a rumour that he'd given up completely and switched to insects, specialising in a genus of flies, *Scatophaga*. Last I heard, someone said that most of the time he goes birding abroad. Alone.

16

The Place that Launched a Thousand Trips

49 Common Nighthawks, Chordeiles minor
Cape May, New Jersey, USA, 11 September 1998

I can completely understand Bob Shutbill's decision to go abroad. Given his peculiar record in the UK he has more to gain than most from foreign birding. Strange as it may seem, stringing requires the relatively narrow hierarchical context in Britain for it to carry meaning. Although most countries now have an indigenous birding community, as a brief visitor Bob can largely bypass the local networks. Even in many European countries, such as Spain or Portugal, he can go a fortnight without meeting a single other member of the tribe.

Without all that competitive baggage about reputation and status, Bob has the chance to be free of his foibles. Alone on foreign soil he'll either lose the desire to do it or, if it's so deep-seated that he just cannot resist pulling a sly one over himself . . . well, who cares? Bob can let rip with impunity. For him birding abroad is a win-win situation.

In fact it's a win-win-win scenario because Bob gains what every other UK birder acquires: access to all the birds that so far haven't made it to Britain. Those 9430 species are spread across the planet's infinite variety of wonderful landscapes. I think of this combination as a holy alliance, a form of heaven on earth, which I first glimpsed twenty-seven years ago, when my parents took me for a two-week package holiday to northern Portugal.

It was August 1974. I somehow knew it was an important moment and commemorated the occasion with a brand-new notebook, number 3, a blue hardback cashbook. I open the fragile childhood document and even now some of it comes flooding straight back: the softly slurred consonants of spoken Portuguese; that first taste of dark, thick-fleshed olives in their own oil; the astringent stink of Mediterranean scrub in the hot summer sun; the sudden, faintly menacing rustle of a lizard, fizzing through the undergrowth like a lighted fuse.

Then I turn to page two and there they are: lists of birds, Portuguese birds, Mediterranean standards, at which I would now barely look twice, like Fan-tailed Warbler, Sardinian Warbler, Crested Lark, Melodious Warbler and Spotless Starling. Yet at the time they seemed extraordinary and exciting discoveries. Most were rare or even unrecorded in Britain; in two weeks I saw more new species than I'd seen at home all year. It signalled the beginning of the end for part of my birding motivation.

When we go abroad it eventually dawns on some of us, why expend huge amounts of time, money and energy on birds that are rare in Britain, but easily seen elsewhere? Why dash overnight to the Scillies (as thousands did in 1998) for Britain's first Spotless Starling (which turned out to be an aberrant Common Starling), when you can enjoy the burble and wheeze of a singing male from your Portuguese hotel balcony? Why lament the missing of the last British Houbara Bustard, when you can savour the madness of its display beneath the hot spring sun of the Negev Desert? Why thrash vainly to Donna Nook for a bogus Black Lark if you can hear the genuine article, its rich mimetic trill rolling to the horizon on the steppes of Kazakhstan?

In Britain it's taken Ron Johns fifty years to see 545 species. Abroad, in Peru, say, or Kenya you can see 540 during a week. In Britain you'd be lucky to see 340 species in any one year; John Fanshawe and Terry Stevenson saw 342 birds on a single day in Kenya, the highest total ever achieved anywhere in the world. With countries that lack a developed ornithological tradition there is, perhaps, less of a sense of history or theatre. Benin is one place I've visited that feels like an ornithological *terra nullius* (in truth it isn't). But in many ways it's a purer experience. It's just you and the birds. The whole impact of foreign birding strikes at the heart of a birder's British preoccupations. Abroad spoils us and we can never be the same again.

In a sense world birding is nothing new. British birders have been going overseas for the last two centuries and have played a major role in the development of ornithology across half the planet. The difference between then and now, however, is in the style of travel and the social make-up of the people involved.

Previously those birders who went overseas were members of the shooting and fishing fraternity – essentially colonial administrators and officers in the armed forces. Their foreign postings were usually a result of imperial policy. Their birding activities had official status, their expeditions were backed by local government, financed with serious money and manned by hundreds of servants. Half the time most of the bird work was actually done by an army of bearers, hunters, collectors, skinners and scribes. A Victorian like Brian Hodgson even trained 'native' artists to do his bird paintings for him. As late as the 1950s some of the old guard were still birding in this fashion. Colonel Richard Meinertzhagen made a private expedition around Arabia in 1951 as a guest of Ibn Saud and when Meinertzhagen needed help moving his mountains of equipment around, the king obliged with one of his private planes.

If modern birding abroad has any antecedents at all, it's with some of the parvenus who broke into that upper-class cartel in the nineteenth century – men like Henry Bates and the great Alfred Russel Wallace. Bates was the son of a hosier, Wallace was a working-class orphan who left school at thirteen. In their early twenties the two men financed a four-year expedition to Amazonia by collecting specimens across the zoological spectrum and then shipping them home to be sold to museums and collectors. When Wallace sailed back to England, Bates stayed on in South America for another seven years, but his former partner then did an eight-year stint in south-east Asia. Wallace's final collection from the trip included 128,000 specimens.

By the mid-twentieth century the trade in scientific material had ended, but new opportunities have since given thousands of birders access to the rest of the planet. In fact, if you look at the evolution of birding into a popular pastime, it serves as a perfect mirror for a number of socio-economic developments in Britain during the last half-century. The expanded ownership of expensive consumer durables (cars, optics, even books) the increase in leisure time and surplus income are all implicated in the process. Similarly the expansion of world birding into a broad-based multi-million-pound pursuit runs in exact parallel with the growth of mass tourism.

Even so, it seems of a piece with birders' obsessive drives that they should be such committed wanderers, in fact one of Britain's last nomadic tribes. By the standards of friends, my own record is modest but it half illustrates the point. Since that fortnight in Viana do Castelo a quarter of a century ago I've been abroad sixty times, almost all of them for birds. This includes visits to thirty-five countries, about a quarter of them in sub-Saharan Africa. That country total doesn't include visits to the Falkands (twice), the Galapagos, four Greek islands (seven visits), the Canaries, Ascencion Island or birding from the loo in Addis Ababa airport. It comes to a total of well over three years on foreign soil. A third of it has been spent in India and Nepal, mainly the Himalayas. About half was during the years 1978 and 1984, between the ages of eighteen and twenty-four.

Now let's talk about some serious bird travel and I stress that this is travel, *not* foreign residence. I have four friends who live just across the town in Norwich. They have an average age of thirty-nine. One has been abroad sixty-seven times to twenty-six countries on five continents, including China, Pakistan, Turkey (thirteen times), Cuba (eleven visits), Brazil (five times), Argentina and Colombia (each three times), Ecuador, Chile and Venezuela. The time spent in South America and the Caribbean amounts to thirty months. The total in Turkey alone comes to almost two years.

Another has travelled for a total of nearly six years through thirty-five countries. These embrace four continents, but especially Asia. The countries he's covered extensively include China, India, Japan, Malaysia (six times), Myanmar, Pakistan, Philippines, Sabah, Sikkim, Taiwan, Thailand (eleven times), Tibet, and Vietnam (nine times).

The third has been birding abroad for a total of over five years, with eighteen months in Africa, from Lesotho to Egypt and from Namibia to Morocco. Although he's visited forty-six countries on six continents, South America is a main focus, with more than two years in Argentina, Bolivia, Brazil, Colombia, Ecuador, Peru and Venezuela.

The last of the quartet has a travel record nearing six years, almost half of it in Asia including Assam, Bhutan (three times), China (four visits), Japan, Taiwan, Tibet and Yemen (six visits). While his journeys embrace all continents except Australia, his speciality is islands, including Socotra, the Cape Verdes, Madeira, Madagascar, the Seychelles and Hawaii.

That pattern of constant travel is increasingly commonplace amongst birders. One of its inevitable effects is to disrupt the continuity of your local birding experience. It loosens any concern for the competitive aspects involved with British twitching. Most rein in or give up, while some world birders abandon *any* form of birding activity in this country altogether. But a few try to span both fields. Ron Johns' 100-plus foreign birding trips reflect that ambition, but his recent declaration of semi-retirement from British listing, in order to focus efforts abroad, suggests the difficulties involved.

For others like Chris Batty, however, it can lead to moments of almost unbearable tension. In September 1998 Chris and his mate Kieran were at Cape May, a top American birding location just south of Atlantic City. They'd been there over a week and seen a sack of good birds, when Kieran made the mistake of ringing home. Kieran's mum in St Helens had been left in charge of

Kieran's bird pager. During his ordinary UK existence his pager keeps him informed of all British rare bird sightings. In his absence, however, he'd left the thing set at 'mega-alert', which meant that it would only beep if a major rarity occurred. It had. His mum had to relay the news that there was a Common Nighthawk on St Agnes in Scilly, of which there had been just fourteen in Britain ever.

The last one had been a decade earlier when Chris was in primary school. They sensed that this might be the only British nighthawk opportunity for the next decade, so they rang the airline, rescheduled the flight tickets and had one last day birding around Cape May, before setting out on their long, unforeseen journey to the Scilly Isles. During the course of that final twenty-four hours they saw lots of excellent birds, including a lovely flock of forty-nine graceful creatures hawking over meadows at sunset, whose identity we'll return to shortly.

That night Chris and Kieran walked across the Cape May island between the hours of two and five to catch the dawn bus into Atlantic City, then their connection on to New York. By Monday morning they'd landed at Manchester airport and by Tuesday evening they were stood at Pelistry on the north-east side of St Mary's and it was looking like a total disaster.

Kieran had seen the bird – briefly – but Chris had missed it completely. They'd already had to reschedule their return flights off Scilly that day to give them a few extra hours' birding. Now they'd been there all afternoon and it was going dark. They'd travelled over 3000 miles and hadn't really had a full night's sleep in four days and it still looked as if they were going to dip.

Then, as rare birds sometimes do, the nighthawk showed. It flew past them, then flew towards them and finally swooped and dove directly above their heads for the next fifteen minutes. It was an incredibly beautiful and wonderful sight and one of the most fulfilling birds that Chris had ever seen. But, strangely enough, while it might have been a new British species for him, it didn't really look deeply unfamiliar. You remember those forty-nine birds they'd seen hawking around at Cape May just a few days ago? They were nighthawks too. In other words

Chris had flown back to England from the United States for a bird he'd seen four days earlier.

Few people are torn by quite the same sense of conflict as Chris Batty, but it would be true to say that all world birders face a major and stubborn lifestyle issue. If you set aside the massive commitment and detailed ornithological intelligence on foreign parts as the core prerequisites of world birding, you can see it involves two basic constituents – time and money. Usually it absorbs time and money in sizeable quantities. Most people can manage to solve half the equation. Acquiring a job settles the question of finance. Quitting the job then resolves the shortage of time. But the deep-seated challenge facing world birders is to have both simultaneously.

Nowadays the four Norwich birders I mentioned earlier are able to juggle freelance birding careers to achieve exactly that balance. Yet in the 1970s, when world birding really took off, there were virtually no professional opportunities in birds. A quarter of a century ago the best deal on offer was to go and make money in Shetland.

Not only were they geographically close to Fair Isle, one of Britain's top birding locations, but the Shetlands were awash with money from the oil boom. New buildings and installations were constantly being thrown up as the North Sea oil poured ashore, and this led to a rash of jobs in construction and site maintenance. The casual regime, the unskilled nature of the work and the high wages were perfect for world birders. Sometimes they were earning five times the usual pay in England. They could put aside several thousand pounds in a matter of months. When they'd spent it all after a comparable period birding abroad, another job was usually there for the taking on their return.

There was, of course, a significant price to pay in terms of inconvenience and discomfort. The standard Shetland jobs were hard manual labour – digging ditches in the teeth of northerly gales or humping scaffolding ten hours a day. But there was some scope for variation. One unfortunate, instead of landing on his feet with oil-rich wages, wound up as the cleaner at Lerwick power station. His work day comprised crawling on hands and knees wiping the dirt from the sump with oily rags.

Toilet cleaner was another Shetland standby, but at the oil terminals this vocation offered serious opportunities to make money with minimum exertion. In fact a good deal of the time was spent sitting on your backside reading *British Birds*. The one serious drawback to this particular career was the draughty toilet cubicle, which left the lavatory hygiene operative a martyr to haemorrhoids.

Some birders were more ambitious. One enterprising teen-ager, for instance, set up a maintenance and cleaning company employing his mates as staff. All of them were birders and the ornithological roots of the outfit were enshrined in its name 'Sibe Cleaners'. Even 'Cleaners' has a vague birding connotation, because if you go for three rarities on one twitching trip and see them all, we say you've 'cleaned up'. The managing director, just nineteen, negotiated a number of lucrative deals with building contractors, in which Sibe Cleaners was required to complete the furbishment of various new premises. One was a school and another the new Lerwick job centre.

However, the foundation of the company could perhaps have been timed more carefully. It came into operation just as autumn bird migration was reaching its feverish peak. Almost inevitably the company came to a premature end; I suspect the writing was on the wall the morning that one set of contractors happened to make a site visit to find not a single Sibe Cleaners' employee in the building. They had all flown to Fair Isle that day to see one particularly exciting rarity.

Another shrewd scheme for making money was devised by a birder who worked in a bar attached to the social club at one of the main oil terminals. Two key issues for all those in Shetland were the lack of cheap accommodation and transport to work from the small towns and hamlets on Shetland mainland. The bar worker found a unique solution to both problems. Unbeknown to the other staff, he slept onsite in a linen cupboard. Working twelve-hour shifts, sleeping in a cupboard upstairs, eating and drinking without charge in the bar, he was able to accumulate very rapidly. His only outlay was for a weekly copy of the *New Musical Express*.

There were some interesting close shaves. Once he locked himself out of his cupboard while taking a shower. The one staff member aware of his clandestine residence amongst the sheets and pillowcases possessed the only other key. He had to search for her around the building dressed just in a towel.

Another near miss occurred when Shetland was hit by severe snowstorms. Every day he went through a daily charade of going out of the building the back way, and entering the bar through the front door, as if he had just arrived from his lodgings. On this particular occasion he made an entry through the front as if everything were normal, to find that he was about the only person able to get through the snowdrifts that morning. The management was deeply impressed by his commitment, but couldn't for the life of them work out how he'd managed it. He didn't even have a car.

He lived in the linen cupboard for two stretches of three months, punctuated by a birding trip to Thailand. When he finished he hitched all the way across America to Alaska and finally ended up in California, where he was mugged and lost everything but the clothes he was wearing.

Like all gold rush localities, Shetland in the late 1970s had an air of transience and almost feverish unreality. The lifestyle was a mixture of unaccustomed opulence and destitution. It was also recklessly subversive. It was, in one way, a fulfilment of Mrs Thatcher's corner-shop notions of self-reliance, but in others an absolute denial of everything she stood for. On Thursday evening you could get a pay packet choked with twenty-pound notes, then go home to a mouldy caravan the size of a garden shed, whose only prospect of comfort was a tin of spaghetti hoops and the faltering gas flame from a single ring. The other standard accommodation was a remote croft half an island away from the main oil terminals at Sullom Voe. The work was tough, incredibly tedious and involved long hours and by the mid 1980s most of the jobs had vanished and the birders migrated. Yet, at its height the North Sea oil boom gave rise to an extraordinary moment in birding history.

Most of those who went to Shetland were aged between eighteen and thirty and while all were there to generate money for foreign trips, it was also a massive source of birding *value*. This alone occasions a bitter-sweet regret in me. I feel that to have missed the Barn at Cley was a shame, but to have missed Shetland was a sin. Whenever I hear those wonderful wild old stories I feel like the child, nose pressed against the ice-cold glass, as the rains dance on the puddles outside.

Of course the stories are important to the birders' oral traditions, but I think there was a much wider significance to Shetland. This is partly to do with some of its lasting repercussions in the birding world. Because, although many spent as lavishly as they earned, there are a few what one might call rags-to-riches stories. The birder, for instance, one of the original Shetland pioneers, who didn't just go abroad, he bought part of it, purchasing sections of rainforest while setting up a bar in Cuzco and running a tour company that specialises in Peruvian birds. Chris Kightley also left Shetland with a five-figure sum and eventually created Limosa, one of the most successful bird holiday operations in Britain. A third used his sizeable stash to buy properties and enjoys a life of ornithological leisure secured by his rents.

Yet Shetland's real impact is more than these individual good-luck tales. The period established a pattern, not just in terms of creating money quickly, but in terms of new birding experience. And this affected far more than the few score people who made it to the islands, more even than those others who wanted to be there or still planned to go. (Such was Shetland's allure that one or two abandoned secure positions in the old family firm or a career in banking to get there. Others thought of it as a kind of schooling by itself – a zany hands-on alternative to tertiary education, while some birders actually at university couldn't wait to get their degree out of the way, so they too could hitch north and don the wellies.)

Even those like me who never went there (I've still to catch the *St Clair* out of Aberdeen) were affected by Shetland. It generated so many stories of fantastic journeys: ten-month trans-Asian odysseys through Iran and Afghanistan to Nepal and the Burmese frontiers of India, or round-the-world voyages taking in Thailand, Malaysia, Taiwan and Hawaii. In 1980 who did you know visiting Japan or Guatemala? Those birders who rode the North Sea oil boom set the standard and Shetland, the place that launched a thousand trips, fuelled all our dreams.

17

US Cops and Mexican Bandits

1 Atitlán Grebe, Podilymbus gigas
Lake Atitlán, Guatemala, 28 December 1978

Southern California's finest walked over towards the driver's door, lowered his shades and glared at Clive, the same Clive who had hitched to Vorran Island for the Steller's Eider, the very same Clive who'd been sprayed with manure at the Reading Black-winged Pratincole.

'What *the* HELL dya think yer doing, buddy?' the cop demanded. In the circumstances it was probably fair comment. Clive had just driven away from Los Angeles airport in a hire car without being in possession of a driving licence. But then no one in the car had a driving licence because none of them had passed their test. One had a provisional and two had international licences, the sort you can buy for a couple of quid and the price of a passport photo. The car-hire company had seemed perfectly happy with these, so off they'd shot.

Yet it wasn't the minor infraction over licences that concerned the policeman. What troubled him was the fact that the car had just jumped a red light on the wrong side of the road. Fortunately Clive's English accent and Irish charm seemed to calm the situation, and by themselves probably helped account for the style of driving. The policeman mellowed, offered some fatherly advice, then watched them pull away with a little West Coast hospitality, 'You all take care, now.'

It was a close shave, but things had started more or less as they were set to continue. It was a British birding trip and in many ways it was absolutely typical of the scores of independent foreign holidays that were being organised by birders and launched from Shetland. Although *holiday* is perhaps misrepresenting it a shade. They weren't so much recreational excursions as feverish ornithological missions, an attempt by the tribe to get at the vast world of birds which now seemed to lie open to us.

I should perhaps also admit that *typical* isn't quite accurate either. The quartet stopped by the LA policeman that balmy November afternoon in 1978 were unusual on a number of counts, not least because Britain's offshore islands were disproportionately represented by the foursome. Debbie, the only female, was a native of the Scilly Isles. The three males, meanwhile – Clive, Ray, who was Debbie's boyfriend, and Craig – were all veterans of the Shetland scene. Although in November 1978, *veteran* too was a slight misnomer.

Craig was nineteen. Today he's one of the country's top birders, author of *A Field Guide to the Birds of South-East Asia*, and better travelled in that region than almost any of his fellows. In fact only a handful of people on the planet have seen more birds in Asia. But in 1978 his only foreign experience, apart from family holidays around the Med, was a Leicester Young Birdwatchers trip to the Netherlands.

Ray and Clive were each twenty-one. Despite their youth they already had what one might call an ornithological history. They'd been school pals together in south London and were members of a local Young Ornithologists' Club, a branch of the RSPB devoted to juniors, in which small group they were joined by Dick Filby and Franko Maroevic.

It was a memorable encounter. The best way I can think to convey the scale of coincidence in this historic assembly is to say it was a bit like Lou Reed, Iggy Pop, Mick Jagger and Keith Richards all being in the same school band. Franko was once described in an American birding magazine as a 'devil incarnate'. Ray and Clive were widely known in their teens as the 'Midwitch Cuckoos', after those weird little aliens in John Wyndham's novel. It reflected their vague physical similarity to one another, especially the Aryan blond hair and short stature, and perhaps also the atmosphere of impish humour that seemed to follow them around.

One typical prank was when they got hold of a tape recorder during a coach outing to Minsmere and set up a mock interview with the YOC group leader. But first they pre-recorded on the machine, 'Derek, we understand you're a bit of a wanker. Could you tell us how many times you've done it today?' Then with the microphone concealed, one of them went up to the head man and posed a similar if more innocent enquiry: 'We've seen a lot of Bitterns today, Derek. How many have you seen?'

Unaware of the trap being set, poor old Derek proceeded to recount the day's tally. 'Well, I had one earlier this morning in the public hide, another over by island mere . . . oh, yes, and then, remember, that one we had on the way to island mere . . . That was a very nice one.'

The playback and roars of schoolboy laughter on the back seat were enough to see them go home with letters banning them from further outings. This was quickly followed by a second red card from the Surbiton District Birdwatching Society.

By 1978 Clive and Ray had spread their wings well beyond the range of their old YOC group and after a stint in Shetland they planned the first of several major foreign trips. For US birders, Central America is virtually their own backyard, but for the British at that time an ornithological sweep all the way from California to Panama was ambitious stuff. Very few had ever been there. It would put Clive, Craig, Debbie and Ray within range of well over a thousand species of bird and they needed no more incentive to hit the trail.

The original plan involved returning the hire car as soon as they'd bought a replacement vehicle. This turned out to be a stroke of real luck – most of it bad – a big dark blue Chevrolet Malibu '68 with racing wheels, snapped up for $800 from a dealer in Hollywood. This bargain perfectly suited the trip budget. Although they had all been earning serious wages on Shetland, money was tight for at least one of them. Part of the original economy drive was a decision to do without one or two minor luxuries that less adventurous souls might perhaps have elected not to forgo. Fripperies such as, well . . . insurance on the vehicle, additional tax once the existing disc expired and an exhaust pipe.

To be honest, the exhaust was one of the few bits of the car that had been dodgy even when they bought it. While they'd initially tied it up with string, it kept working loose and was eventually ripped off altogether. Thereafter this contingent of British birders roared across Central America in a Malibu '68 that sounded like a jumbo jet. Ultimately they concluded they could also do perfectly well without the racing tyres. So when some hot-rod took a shine to their wheels in a Mexican bar, they negotiated a swap for his own four, plus a few pesos on top.

But now I'm getting ahead of myself. Even before the hire car was returned and the Malibu bought, the birding had got off to a flier. Overnight they'd driven for the first really big bird of the trip. The following morning they spotted a California Condor soaring over the peaks flanking Sespe Creek in Ventura County. It wasn't a particularly great view, but then these birds are notoriously difficult to observe closely. They tend to range over huge areas and this makes their movements unpredictable. Today even that distant sighting by itself would justify the entire trip.

The California Condor is a big bird in every sense. The heaviest weigh over twenty pounds and have a wingspan in excess of nine feet, although its Andean cousin is even larger, in fact the biggest raptor in the world. But what gives the North American bird an unparalleled status is extreme rarity.

For tens, if not hundreds, of thousands of years the California Condor had followed the huge herds of megafauna roaming the wilds of North America. However as these died out, in the extinction bottlenecks created by successive ice ages, so the bird's range began to shrink. Even before the arrival of Europeans on the continent the condor was probably already confined to the West Coast. By the time Clive, Craig, Debbie and Ray arrived in the land of the free, this Pleistocene relic was down to the wire. In the late 1970s there were two or three dozen left. In 1981 a census revealed three breeding pairs. By 1985 there was just one. By 19 April 1987 all of the last few California Condors had been taken into protective custody, housed mostly in San Diego zoo.

Over a decade later the captive stock is doing well and a few of them have even been re-released. But these free-flying birds are hardly independent. They're fed on specially provided 'clean' carcasses, their movements are monitored by radio transmitter and, if necessary, the birds are recaptured for a refit and service. They are, in effect, glorified cagebirds. No birder who's seen the species post 1987 can put hand on heart and claim to have seen a wild condor. In fact some doubt whether they can ever adapt to the conditions of modern California or be truly considered 'wild' again, certainly not for the next few generations. In terms of the condor's inexorable spiral down through the millennia towards extinction, Clive, Craig, Debbie and Ray had just shaved it again.

With the condor seen, the Malibu now bought and loaded, the gang of four roared out of California, across Arizona and New Mexico and into Texas for another five-star US bird. For much of the twentieth century the Whooping Crane had followed the condor into extinction's borderland – by 1941 it hit an all-time low of sixteen birds – but with major help from pioneer environmentalists it had then turned itself around. In 1978 this magnificent snow-white crane, the continent's tallest bird, was relatively common compared to the condor, with at least seventy left on the planet (today there are over 400). Even so, it was one of the target species and when Clive and the others bumped into a handful at a wintering site known as Aransas National Wildlife Refuge just south-east of San Antonio on the Gulf of Mexico, it was one of the trip's key encounters. Now even greater riches lay across the border.

With a strategically placed 'donation', an uninsured, taxless, exhaust-free Malibu '68 eased its way across the border at Brownsville. This opened up a whole month of birding through Mexico. They moved in a long, slow arc around the country's Gulf coast, through Tampico, Puebla, Oaxaca and on into Campeche, Yucatan and Cozumel. Then, after Mexico, lay Belize and Guatemala.

It is a strange and fascinating coincidence that birds are often concentrated around ancient monuments of spiritual or archaeological importance: Delphi in Greece, Petra in Jordan or India's Taj Mahal are all good examples. It's as if these wonderful human artefacts and the abundance of wildlife honour the same great upwelling of life at the one spot. The Mayan ruins of Tikal, Uxmal and Palenque are all representative of the same phenomenon. So as Clive, Craig, Ray and Debbie toured the key locations of Mesoamerican civilisation they encountered an extraordinary array of Neotropical birds.

I know that had I been on that trip almost a quarter of a century ago the whole spectrum of bird experience from that month would have distilled down to a single memory collage, like a great Rivera mural, crowded with colour and intensity. One of the few palpable mementoes, of course, is the notebook. Just the lists of birds by themselves conjure something of those days birding dawn to dusk: Violaceous Trogon, Turquoise-browed Motmot, Rufous-tailed Jacamar, Emerald Toucanet, White-whiskered Puffbird, Ivory-billed Woodcreeper, Scaly-throated Foliage-gleaner, Rose-throated Becard, Rufous-browed Peppershrike, Red-legged Honeycreeper, Flame-coloured Tanager, Montezuma Oropendula. These alone seem like treasures, syllables filled with a sense of the other. Birding in the tropics isn't just the pursuit of a hobby or the fulfilment of an obsession; at times it seems like a quest for life itself as expressed through bird sound, bird movement, bird colour. For me it has no equal in all ornithology.

Towards the end of the trip the group finally reached the northern Guatemalan province of Petén. However, the route to Tikal, their ultimate goal, was so bad they were forced to leave the Malibu at the roadside and take a local bus to the celebrated Mayan ruins. After their three-day visit they retraced their steps to the car, then headed off for Guatemala City and one of their last destinations further to the west, a site called Lake Atitlán.

The primary objective was to see a seriously rare species, *Podilymbus gigas*, known more memorably as Giant Pied-billed Grebe or, more simply, as Atitlan Grebe (it occurred nowhere else in the world than the single volcanic lake of that name). Although best of all is the local Guatemalan name, *Poc*. The monosyllabic brevity captures something essential about the bird. It sounds like a full stop.

It was the third of the trip's extreme rarities. California Condor, Whooping Crane and Atitlan Grebe were all classified as Endangered, the highest category of threat in the system used to grade the world's most vulnerable species. But had you been a betting man in 1978 you might have put odds on the grebe at least to outlast the vulture. In the late 1970s the estimated total of 200-plus birds was significantly higher than for either of the other species.

True, the grebe was vulnerable. It was thought that the world total had never exceeded 400 birds. It was flightless and confined to one small lake. It was highly dependent on a single prey item – freshwater crabs – to deal with which it had acquired a large muscular head and powerful bill. An earthquake in the area in 1976 had caused water levels on Lake Atitlán to fall and there were threats from a proposed hydro-electric scheme. Even so, the grebe's extinction by the mid 1980s was sudden and dramatic. It's one of only a handful of species to vanish in my lifetime. No one could have predicted that when Clive, Craig and the others saw it close inshore on 28 December 1978, they would be amongst the last Britons ever to see the bird alive.

The main cause of its demise was genetic swamping by the closely allied pan-American Pied-billed Grebe. Interbreeding with this relative hybridised the larger single-lake endemic into oblivion. Based on this evidence some maintain that *Podilymbus gigas* wasn't actually a full species, merely a distinctive race of the other bird. Whatever the merits of the argument, the Atitlan Grebe is no more.

Not that Clive and Craig could have known the significance of the sighting at the time. Even if they had, it might not have concerned them. They now had other things to worry about. Shortly after seeing the grebe, Craig left the car in the middle of the night to go to the loo and when he woke in the morning, there was no sign of his wallet or his air ticket. The only thing they could think was that they had fallen out of his pocket as he squatted by the roadside. By first light next morning there was a stream of passers-by walking along the road and the likeliest explanation is that some lucky Guatemalan had found a pile of gringo scat with a £200 wad next to it.

Craig now had no ticket and no money. That was enough bad luck for one trip, but he'd already been robbed in eastern Guatemala. They'd actually seen the thieves driving off from the Malibu, but had been too late to stop them breaking into the car and nicking his jean jacket. That was a drag but Craig, nineteen, on his first trip in the Third World, had left his passport in the pocket.

On 24 December, before heading for Lake Atitlán, he had finally managed to persuade the disgruntled British consul in Guatemala City to issue him with a replacement. The guy had been so hacked off to have his Christmas Eve disturbed by a dishevelled, importunate nineteen-year-old birder that when he finally whacked it with the seal, he cut a hole straight through the paper. It meant that by New Year's Eve, Craig had no money, no ticket and a passport whose validation stamp was forever falling out.

Things were looking bad for him. His one consolation, perhaps, was the reflection that matters weren't too hot for Clive either. He'd run out of money even before Craig's disaster. I suspect it might be true to say that finances have never been a strong point with Clive. His standard tactic on later tours was to have an expensive set of optics or camera, which he could sell to tide him over. In Guatemala, however, the plan was to borrow from Craig.

Now both of them were skint and the tour was unravelling fast. Any hope of reaching Panama had faded completely. Besides, the Malibu was a wreck and the tyres were bald. While Craig and Clive had always planned to split from the others, now it was essential. Ray and Debbie managed to scrape together an emergency surplus of about fifty quid for them, a sum which would have to see the two destitutes back to Los Angeles, a small matter of 2500 miles.

On New Year's Eve, Ray and Debbie drove them to the border and, after final farewells, set off to make their own slow route back to California up the west coast of Mexico. For Clive and Craig there was only one familiar transport option. Hitch.

Then they had a stroke of luck . . . almost all of it bad. Three guys stopped in a van and offered to take to them all the way from Oaxaca to Mexico City, from where they could easily catch a bus back to Texas. That was fine. The less fortunate part was being cooped up for most of the twelve-hour journey in the covered rear of the vehicle. Even worse was the fact that through the rear glass panel they could observe the behaviour of their three drivers. One of the Mexican customs for seeing out the old year seemed to involve passing round the whisky and tequila while taking turns at the wheel. Clive and Craig could already see the obituary section of *British Birds*:

DRUNKEN PILE-UP IN OAXACA
TWO ENGLISH BIRDERS . . .

Towards midnight they finally found themselves cruising through the endless suburbs of Mexico City. The two in the back could at last let out a 500-mile-long sigh of relief. And after dropping off his mates, the owner of the van, in a last gesture of international friendship, invited his gringo pals back to the house for a celebratory nerve-soothing drink. It was a welcome act of kindness and all the more touching because home proved to be a one-room shanty complete with communal bed, grandma and a host of doe-eyed infants.

He poured the tequilas. They offered toasts to the New Year and to Brito-Mexican relations. Warmed now by the strong spirits, moved by their host's genuine kindness, Clive and Craig sat back in the van one last time as he chauffered them to the station. Then, as he set down their bags, as he shook them vigorously by the hand, as he waved his final friendly farewells, the two young birders were filled with that pleasing glow, that sense of global fraternity which – without wishing to sound too conceited on their behalf – comes only to those who have known and shared the travails of long-haul travel.

As they lingered a moment, reflecting on the day's many tribulations and this last act of simple human friendship, Craig happened to notice the strap of his binocular case, hanging limply from the rucksack. That's odd, thought Craig. So he opened the bag to check and found the case empty, which was very odd. Clive did the same. His was empty too. The two looked at one another and they reflected again . . . While they'd stood in his miserable shack, while they'd toasted the New Year, while they'd bantered with granny and fooled with the kids, their Mexican friend had feigned a visit to the toilet, gone to the vehicle, opened their bags, nicked the binoculars, closed the bags and, cool as you like, driven them to the station to wave a fond farewell . . . the BASTARD!

There was nothing for it. They had just enough money to get the Greyhound to El Paso. Even so they had no idea how they were going to make it back to LA, let alone the UK. There were also lesser hurdles. In Cuidad Juarez, the town facing El Paso on the south side of the Rio Grande, Craig had to visit the American consulate to get his new two-part passport stamped with a fresh American visa.

Then, on their way to the border crossing itself, something rather remarkable happened. Although in the context of this particular trip you may well possibly accept it as a more routine occurrence. Clive, having just looked at his own passport in the American consulate, suddenly discovered it was now missing along with his air ticket. For this miraculous disappearance they could think of only two explanations. Someone had picked his pocket on the bus, or the friendly guy who happened to stop and speak with them on the street had mingled his moment of back-slapping with a surreptitious hand inside Clive's jacket pocket. This was the border town, after all.

Either way, he was confronted with a fresh dilemma. There he was, at the beginning of the bridge. Just across this single structure was the United States, complete with its promise of charity and collect-call pay phones and money transfers. For now, however, Clive, on the south side of the Rio Grande, minus money *and* passport *and* the will to put up with it any longer, turned to Craig and said, 'I've had enough, I'm going to go for it.'

Getting past the Mexican guard was a doddle and he was soon out in no man's land breezing down the bridge towards America. In fact Craig could see his friend, a little blond-haired figure way off in the distance. Ten minutes later there he was again, ashen and drained in the custody of Texas's finest.

'Buddy,' said the border guard at the moment of seizure, 'yurrr in BIG trouble!' But for Clive trouble was now a relative term. In fact, it turned out to be less serious than it appeared. A mere incarceration, a call to the Irish consulate in Chicago, and he was a free man with the requisite visa and document. Within a few hours they'd hitched all the way from El Paso in Texas to Los Angeles in California, most of the 800 miles in a Beetle, whose driver spent the journey either rolling joints or trying to pick women up over his CB radio.

For the first few days, until the tickets came through, they tried a Jesus Loves You mission in downtown LA. It was a huge single-room dormitory filled every night with about 400 drop-outs and dead-beats. The winos kept bottling one another and drunken Indians were at each others' throats for the price of a can of Bud. Yet the thing that really got to Clive and Craig was the daily search for crabs and body lice. Another key moment came when a tramp hobbled into the mission shod only in copies of the *Los Angeles Times*, which he proceeded to peel off, revealing two unrecognisable stumps covered in leprotic scabs. When a born-again tramp leapt up on stage declaring his love for Jesus and asked Clive and Craig to testify to the healing powers of the Lord, they could take it no longer.

During their week's wait at the airport they made a visit to the LA beach to go birding with the naked eye (Surf Scoter, Forster's Tern, etc.). A few days later and they were back in England. Three weeks and Clive and Craig were on Shetland, where there were good jobs for the taking on a new Barratt's estate. Twelve months later both of them were off with Ray and two others on a six-month round-the-world trip including Nepal, Thailand, Malaysia, Taiwan, Japan and then back to California.

Shortly after arriving in Kathmandu, Craig made a visit with two of the others to a mountain called Phulchowki just outside the city. They each stashed a heavy rucksack in the bushes while they went off for the day's birding. When they got back one of the bags – *only* one of them – had been stolen. Craig's.

18

Satyr Tragopan, II – the end

1 male Satyr Tragopan, Tragopan satyra
(calling) Tharepati, Nepal, 14 May 1983

The sunlight fell across the dormitory floor in a regular pattern of warm orange lozenges and through the open window the sounds of an Indian winter's evening came pouring in. After just a week in the country they were beginning to seem almost familiar, even comforting – the endless background shrieking from flocks of Rose-ringed Parakeets, the plangent, hoarse notes of milling House Crows and the sound of spoken Hindi echoing down the corridor of the guesthouse.

It was 7 December 1982 and I was at Sarus Lodge, a cavernous government-run accommodation just on the edge of northern India's most famous bird site, the Keoladeo Ghana National Park, better known to its visitors as Bharatpur after the nearby town in northern Rajasthan. As on the previous five days I'd risen at dawn to go birding along the raised banks that divide the large artificial wetland into a series of extensive shallow pools known as jheels. But even by the park entrance I realised this was to be a morning of rest – enforced rest. Day eight of the trip and India had struck in ways familiar to most foreign visitors.

Although to blame my debilitating condition entirely on India was unfair. They were partly the symptoms of self-inflicted exhaustion. I'd been birding hard for the last week, dawn till dusk, subsisting on a single hot meal in the evening, with bananas and a handful of peanuts for lunch. The shortcomings of the regime were now exposed. I pedalled lamely back to the lodge and climbed into a dormitory bed for the rest of the day.

Yet there was an element in this fatigue which I could put down to India's impact. A week of insomnia was the result of feelings of panic and disorientation that had assailed me even as I disembarked from the plane at Delhi airport. I recognise now that the first thing to unsettle me was the unmistakable yet deeply ambiguous odour of India, which always strikes me as part delicate sweetness, part decay. Another indefinable menace seemed to emanate from the country's sheer redness.

There was the brilliant ochre of the earth itself, the fiery orange of Delhi's evening sky. Even the walls of the airport were stained with what looked like congealed gobbets of blood and amongst the press of human faces confronting me in the terminal I quickly recognised the same shade of crimson staining most men's lips and teeth. I didn't know then that much of India's redness derives from its addiction to betel nut. At the time the blood-stained mouths and the colour of the soil seemed all of a piece, as if I'd just arrived in a landscape of the Apocalypse.

After two days milling around Delhi, organising aspects of the trip and fending off feelings of physical and psychological invasion, I decided to head south for the Bharatpur sanctuary. Unfortunately nothing in my first forty-eight hours had quite prepared me for the ordeal of an Indian railway station.

A sea of humanity surrounded it on all sides, and the mass condensed further as we pressed towards the labyrinth of platforms in a seething tide of bodies. Just to disentangle myself from this sprawling amorphous organism and find the spot where the Bharatpur train was due to arrive seemed like a victory in itself, although any sense of achievement was instantly abolished by the appearance of the train.

Brakes squealing frantically, it ground into the crowded station like a monster in pain. When it finally halted at the platform I was struck by a new sense of alarm. Did I really have to get on board the thing? The carriages were painted deep brown and their interiors were in darkness. There was no glass in any of the windows. Instead the gloomy cavities were sealed over with thick metal bars. The seats comprised bare wooden boards painted the same brown as the exterior. It looked perfect for moving livestock or prisoners, but as public transport it was a nightmare.

Eventually I summoned the resolve to fight my way on and settled in a window seat, where I adjusted myself and my possessions for the four-hour journey south into Rajasthan. The two facing benches in this section of the carriage filled very quickly with eight people, all male, three on my side, five opposite. I was grateful for the unequal allocation of territory but couldn't work out whether it was out of respect or fear of the foreigner. All I knew was that the five men opposite, even the others next to me, spent the entire journey dozing or scrutinising me with scientific attentiveness. Everything I did – opening my rucksack, looking at a book or a map, just scratching my head or nodding off for a few moments – elicited the same invasive stare.

Gradually I grew accustomed to the probing audience and my attention wandered to the seamless collage streaming past beyond the train window: timeless scenes of a rural humanity and of slow-moving livestock on a late winter's afternoon in India. Eventually all colour drained from the world and it was reduced to a chiaroscuro of looming shadows and the dancing light off open fires. It was hypnotically beautiful and utterly strange and it might have offered me enough time to adjust to the notion of actually being there. It might have permitted the kind of calm reflection necessary to feel positive about the project on which I was just embarking.

It might have done . . . had the train not stopped at some anonymous rural town and my view through the low window been obscured by the torsos of military figures wielding long sticks. Suddenly one of these 'headless' officials grabbed me by the arm, pinning it to the base of the window, while another khaki-clad figure appeared inside and instantly grabbed me by the other arm. Within seconds I was being aggressively frisked by a burly moustachioed policeman.

Heart pounding afresh under India's latest inexplicable assault, I was ordered to burrow my possessions out of my rucksack and pile them on the bench space left by my neighbour's rapid exit. The policeman eventually satisfied himself that I was not in possession of any drugs and vanished almost as swiftly as he'd appeared. Embarrassed and flustered, I wrestled my heap of possessions back into their bag, before the eyes of my neighbours consumed them completely.

When I finally arrived at Bharatpur station I felt exhausted. I flopped into the seat of a bicycle rickshaw and my driver, with legs no thicker than my arms, strained and heaved to set his chariot in motion. Gradually we inched out of the pool of half-light cast by the station lamps and entered the darkness of the Indian night. At that moment my driver turned to me and smiled, presenting the now familiar vision of carious, blood-stained teeth and mouth.

'Where to, baba?' he asked.

I explained that I wanted the Sarus Lodge and off we moved into the night. I hadn't a clue where we were going. For all I knew I was being pedalled into oblivion by a vampire. But one thing I could tell for sure. This journey was going to be tough, possibly too tough.

The original idea had been to visit India and Nepal for as many months as my £440 would allow and to see as many birds as I possibly could in that time. The plan had been to do all this by myself, but it was clear that the scheme was on the edge of my capabilities. And yet, in a way, while I might have been completely unprepared for the challenge, it had been a perfectly logical thing to do.

In the previous four years I had made nine birding trips abroad and covered several countries in the eastern Mediterranean. Then, with Tog as companion, I'd pressed on beyond Europe, sampling the tip of Africa's vast avifauna in Morocco, as far south as the Sahara. The following year we nibbled at Asia, bisecting Turkey as far east as the Iranian border. Twelve months later we were back in the Middle East, looking for desert birds along Israel's Red Sea coast, which then stretched to Sharm el Sheikh at the tip of the Sinai peninsula.

By 1982 there was, in a sense, nowhere left to go but India and Nepal. Russia was out. Iran was embroiled in Islamic revolution. Further east, Afghanistan had sunk into civil war between the Mujahidin and the Russian-backed Marxist government. Pakistan was the nearest possible destination. Yet bird-wise it made no sense.

The Himalayas are ornithologically richer the further east one travels. Technically the optimum destinations would have been Sikkim, Bhutan and the north-east hill-states of India. But in that region you encountered the same kinds of political obstacle to those barring access to Iran and Afghanistan. All factors pointed towards northern India and Nepal, a country which, proportional to surface area, has one of the largest avifaunas on earth.

But there was one further key factor propelling me to this destination and that was my home in Norwich at 104 Unthank Road. An ordinary three-bedroomed Victorian end-terrace on one of the arterial routes radiating out of the city centre, 104 was a kind of ornithological tardis. Utterly insignificant from the outside, it was a dynamo of birding energy within. Almost everybody who lived there was a committed world birder. In fact half the people mentioned in this book either stayed or visited periodically at 104. The house had only seven small rooms, but it routinely held as many as a dozen individuals enjoying various degrees of temporary residency.

None of this was probably very unusual for a university house. What marked 104 out from other Norwich undergraduate places was the cultural ethos. If you'd entered other student houses in the early 1980s you'd probably have uncovered conversations about who was having the party this weekend, or the best local spot for magic mushrooms, or the latest Clash album. Those with intellectual pretensions may have roiled under Thatcher's butchery of student grants, or willed the collapse of international capitalism once Brazil reneged on its World Bank debts.

At 104 none of that mattered. We were more consumed by the tarsal streaks on Bruce's Scops Owl, or whether you could tell Hume's Yellow-browed Warbler on call. A major point of discussion was the best site in Delhi for Brook's Leaf Warbler. Virtually everyone in the house had been birding in Nepal, some of them several times. I can say in all honesty that even before I'd set foot in the country I knew the topography and place names of the Jomossom trek – the route that runs through the deepest valley in the world towards the Tibetan border – better than the centre of London.

Anyone else who'd recently returned to Britain from a birding trip to the subcontinent seemed to feel impelled to visit us at 104, almost as if it were the last place in their Asian itinerary. Then we'd be treated to the obligatory slide talk on the trip, with endless reminiscences about Kathmandu and its cake shops and bird-sites with names like Hangatham, Ghorepani, Muktinath and Kosi Barrage. In the end I came to hate those slide talks.

All those wonderful-sounding bird names like Greater Scaly-bellied Wren-Babbler and Fire-tailed Myzornis and Satyr Trago-pan were only wonderful if you'd seen them yourself. Even if you *hadn't* seen them, the fact that you'd actually been to look meant that at least you could join in the conversation with a genuine sense of agony. My position in such discussions was completely perverse. I found myself feeling jealous of another man's failure, but at least he'd been there.

By 1982 and the end of my degree there was only one thing for it. I had to go too. But let's be clear. Going to India and Nepal was as much about joining in the debate at the Lily Langtry pub on Unthank Road as it was about a lifetime's adventure. So, you see, in a curious sense, as I lay on my bed at the Sarus Lodge, alone and exhausted, on 7 December 1982, I was partly motivated by a wish to belong. As evening fell, as those warm orange lozenges faded from the dormitory floor and the last parakeets had gone to roost, it no longer seemed such a clear and meaningful goal.

Fortunately all that was just about to change. My first inkling of something new was a great bang as the dormitory door suddenly flew open, followed by a huge black Doc Marten boot. A wiry European figure then materialised in the doorway, labouring under an oversized rucksack and struggling as if in the final triumphant moments of a fight which, in fact, was the case. He had just battled his way from Delhi in much the same sense of panic as I had a week earlier.

Despite the suddenness and drama of the entrance, the vision before me was a deeply familiar figure. It was Alan Adams, an English birder I'd known for years. I suspect our warm greeting, natural in such alien surroundings, was all the warmer because of the deep feelings of relief on both sides. The sense of a whole new trip through India instantaneously opened up before me. Or, rather, I should say before *us*.

Through the grapevine I'd known that Alan was coming to India, just as he knew I was. But there had been no co-ordination or correspondence beforehand. Our meeting was a matter of pure chance. It was the luckiest thing that happened to me in the whole six months.

Alan Adams was a wiry, tousle-headed lad, about a year younger than me and part of a group of keen young birders whose sense of their own forward thrust was commemorated in their nickname, 'The Upstarts'. But Alan was an upstart merely by reputation. Everyone agrees he was a really lovely guy.

He was a Liverpudlian and deeply attached to his regional identity. Whenever he had to explain to Asians where he came from, he always spoke of his home city with great feeling. I can remember him telling one Indian how he lived *very* close to the area of Toxteth that had just then experienced tremendous civil disturbances. The fact that these were Liverpudlian riots meant that Alan afforded them the same sense of civic pride that he showed to any other aspect of the city, like the Beatles or Liverpool FC.

Like almost all scousers, whenever he opened his mouth the things he said seemed to be tinged with an almost unavoidable humour. But he wasn't necessarily a wit, he was more of an enthusiast. While he was bright and articulate, he seldom seemed to be able to find the language to express the passions just then consuming him. When he said he hated something you understood the depth of feeling as much from the effort that went into the words as the language itself.

In truth he didn't often tell you his dislikes. It was much more often the things he loved. He had a large canon of superlatives, which culminated with his own unique phrase. If something was really *really* amazing then Alan described it as 'the end'. Satyr Tragopan was, of course, 'the end'. Kathmandu was 'the end'. Grace Jones's latest album was 'the end'. But it was an expression that could depend on context. A really great cup of tea at a critical moment might also be 'the end'.

The other characteristic of Alan's that I remember most vividly was his laugh. It was bit like his favourite choice of superlatives, a minimalist affair. It consisted largely of an uncontrollable silence punctuated by a short throaty syllable, which is difficult to render in words but is most closely suggested by the letter 'A' repeated at intervals. *Aa-Aa-Aa-Aa-Aa-Aa.* The longer the gaps, the deeper the laughter. Sometimes it could go on for minutes at a time. It was a wonderful sound and I can remember clearly an occasion when we were on a coach out of Kathmandu. Alan's laugh had everyone on the bus staring at us.

But we didn't care. And that, in a nutshell, was the difference that Alan's company made to my trip to India. His presence completed that sense of belonging. We were the tribe. We talked endlessly about birds and birders. It created an entirely familiar world, like a permanent bubble of oxygen around us, through whose filter we could accept the exotic otherness of our surroundings. From being strange and threatening, they suddenly became wonderful and compelling. To this day India and Nepal are my favourite destinations.

After a further week at Bharatpur, Alan and I moved south to the tiger sanctuary near Ranthambhor, then out on to the fringes of the Thar Desert, beyond Jaisalmer. Christmas Day was spent in Delhi and I remember shoving Peter Matthiessen's *Snow Leopard* into Alan's sock while he slept. The New Year was spent in Corbett National Park, on the edge of the Indian Himalayas, and by mid-January we were in Kathmandu.

The culmination of our trip was a six-week walk towards the Tibetan border, the legendary Jomossom trek. We budgeted about £60 for the entire forty-eight-day trip. One of the highlights was a site called Ghasa, renowned as the one spot in the country where you could see all of Nepal's six pheasants, including Satyr Tragopan. We arrived with huge expectations, but gradually they were worn down by the endless steep ascents up the surrounding mountains. We stayed for a week and each morning we trudged breathlessly toward the stands of bamboo, high on the distant slopes that were visible from our lodge window. Once we'd reached the spot, our lodge could then be seen, reduced by distance to the size of a doll's house. But there were seldom pheasants, least of all Satyr Tragopan.

The nearest we came was when our lodge host showed us a male that his father had shot and stuffed. Even that was exciting. The moment was duly celebrated with a series of photographs. I have one of them on the desk now as I write. It shows Alan holding the magnificent blood-red bird with outstretched wings, its lifeless head resting on his breast.

But the failure to find the living creature and four months of continuous day-after-day birding were beginning to take their toll. We never fell out and the closest we came to an argument was a disagreement over religion. Alan, an atheist, condemned institutionalised faiths on the grounds that they caused too many wars and too much suffering. I disagreed, blaming the conflict on an inherent human instinct towards tribalism, of which religious division was merely a symptom.

By the time we got back to Kathmandu in late March I'd had enough of birding and went to stay in a Tibetan monastery just outside the city. But Alan already had his religion. As a birder he was utterly devoted and irrepressible. He went back by himself all the way to Nepal's eastern border, retracing a route we'd taken earlier in the winter. In April he was in the lowlands, at Nepal's premier national park, Chitwan. In May, as I made plans to return home via India's holy city of Varanasi, Alan set out on the Gosainkund–Langtang trek with two friends, Clive and Toby, recently arrived in Kathmandu.

They'd walked for a couple of days and on the day after Black Friday May 1983 they reached a site on an uninhabited ridge at almost 12,000 feet called Tharepati. It had been a gruelling climb and when they arrived in the late afternoon, Toby and Clive decided to rest in a shepherd's hut and make some dinner. But Alan was itching to get out birding. They could hear Satyr Tragopan calling and he was desperate to go and look. He set off at around five in the evening and, as far as we know, that is the last that anyone saw of Alan Adams alive.

If this book makes anything clear, it's the fact that birders will go to whatever lengths it takes in order see birds. The drive that gripped Alan that stormy night in the Himalayas can carry us into all sorts of situations. Most of the time the stories engendered add to the great canon of harmless eccentricities. But in some instances the birder's drive can lead to dreadful tragedy.

Bryan Bland's home, Flanders, is on the main street in Cley and the back of the house overlooks the marsh near to the village's famous mill (the one that appears routinely on the BBC as one of the interlude landscapes shown between programmes). However, a recently dug borrow pit was just out of sight from any of Flanders' existing windows, which was particularly irksome when a Ferruginous Duck appeared on the pool in the winter of 1997. Bryan needed the rare bird for his garden list, which was just approaching 200 species, so he took what he considered the appropriate rational steps. This involved digging a hole through the plaster and the lath, then removing the tiles from his bedroom roof so that he could look out. In the twelve days of Christmas he watched routinely from the new vantage point and saw not only the Ferruginous Duck, but Red-necked Grebe, Great White Egret, American Wigeon, Bittern, Barn Owl and Kingfisher.

On 16 August 1973 Bryan rang his great friend, Pete Milford, to tell him about a European Roller present at East Hills, an isolated patch of pine-topped sand dune to the north of Wells-next-the-Sea on the Norfolk coast. Although visible from Wells's seafront, East Hills is cut off by a maze of creeks and the usual means of access is by boat or a two or three hour circuitous walk over the saltmarsh. The only short route on foot is across the Wells channel at ebb tide when the water comes up to a man's thigh. Outside the brief low-water period the crossing is broad, deep and potentially treacherous.

Pete took his chances at slack water to cross comfortably to East Hills. He then saw the Roller, on the last of its nine-day stay in Norfolk, only to find that the creek had completely filled by his return. Nothing daunted, he tied his binoculars to the top of his head with his belt and set off to swim the 150 yards across the channel. As he approached halfway a speed boat towing a water-skier steamed into the channel. Presumably the boat's driver had never expected a swimmer so far from dry land and they shaved past Pete's head, missing him by inches.

When he finally reached the other side, the families making sand castles gave some very strange looks to the man just emerged from the tide's edge with binoculars strapped to the top of his head.

Cliff Waller is one of the tribe's senior warriors, a long time warden of Walberswick, the famous National Nature Reserve on the Suffolk coast. Even in his early sixties he is a well-built athletic man with a bushy, spade-like beard that gives him a vaguely Islamic air.

In 1970 he was in Afghanistan on an Oxford University expedition to study bird migration through the Himalayas and Hindu Kush. One morning he set out with a friend to walk up the side of a steep canyon and out on to the stony desert plateau above. As birders often do, the two men drifted in separate directions during the course of the morning and lost one another. Cliff decided to make his independent route back to the expedition base camp, situated at an altitude of about 8000 feet near the village of Band-i-Amir.

He was descending through a narrow gorge which cut down the side of the canyon towards the town when he had that eerie horror-film sensation that he was being followed. Dashing forward and climbing a large rock he looked back along his own route to see two Afghani horsemen, poised with rifle in hand, chests criss-crossed with bandoleers and palms pressed firmly over each horse's nose to silence the beasts.

Cliff, sensing the danger, tried to lure his pursuers deeper into the gorge before he scrambled as quickly as he could up a steep slope, which led back to the plateau above and which he knew the bandits' mounts would never negotiate. As he raced up the incline, bullets whined off the rocks nearby and he could see his assailants mount their horses and ride hell for leather back up the gorge.

As soon as Cliff reached the plateau he raced across the open ground for about 700 yards with the bandits in pursuit. Bullets ricocheted off the desert floor kicking up vile little clouds of dust. He'd cut a diagonal route across the edge of the canyon and eventually he had nowhere to go but back down the canyon side. Without a moment's hesitation, without looking back, the sound of horses' hooves pounding the earth behind and fearful for his life, he leapt fifteen feet down a sheer drop then scrambled further down the cliff face beneath an overhanging rock.

The run, probably at an altitude of around 9000 feet, had been totally exhausting (in fact for days afterwards Cliff suffered from altitude sickness as a consequence of the exertion). Through his own gulping breaths he could hear the horses stomping and snorting as they pawed the cliff edge above and the voices of the two men as they discussed their victim's apparent disappearance.

For what seemed like an eternity he waited, unable to go back up in case the bandits were there. Below him was a sheer canyon plunging down 600–700 feet. Mercifully Cliff had been warden on Lundy and assistant on Fair Isle. A good deal of the summer months was spent clambering around the rocks ringing cliff-nesting seabirds. The training now saved his life. Even so, his hands were bruised and painful from wedging them into narrow clefts. On one or two occasions he doubted whether he'd ever make it. It took him hours to reach the bottom and when he got down he walked several miles back to camp in the pitch dark.

David Hunt was a talented, jovial, larger-than-life figure who'd once played the trombone in a backing band to the Rolling Stones. But he was much better known as a birder than as a jazz musician, eventually setting himself up as the RSPB representative resident on Scilly.

On 23 February 1985 David was leading a wildlife holiday group in Corbett National Park in northern India. The group was on elephant back when a large owl flew across their path and disappeared into a forest thicket.

Not one to let such a prize slip, David descended from the howdah and followed the direction of the bird across a rise 150 yards away. The group waited patiently for his return and some of them claim that at one point they may have heard a scream. Whether this was true or not, their armed Indian guide realised that after twenty minutes something was seriously wrong and followed David's route into the bushes, where he found the Englishman mauled to death by a tiger.

The group rushed back to the park's main tourist lodge, roused every available guard, mahout and elephant and returned as fast as they could to retrieve David's body. Such was the state of tiger politics in India in the mid-1980s that a slightly doctored story was put out that he had been killed by a female defending her cubs.

David Hunt was a very gifted photographer and when they retrieved his body and possessions, they eventually took his last film for development. It showed a tiger in all its glory, the shots increasing in quality and drama from the moment of encounter to the point of the great cat's charge. It was, in fact, a male, a creature said to be one of Mrs Gandhi's favourites. It subsequently attacked a member of the park staff and ended its days in Lucknow zoo.

Tim Andrews was one of the keenest world birders in Britain. By 1990 he'd seen close to half the world's species and he was still only thirty. His trip to South America with Mike Entwistle was his fourth major tour after visiting Nepal and India, then Ecuador and, thirdly, Australia with Indonesia and Papua New Guinea.

The second South American trip was an epic. By April 1990 they'd already covered some of the Caribbean islands, such as Puerto Rico, then Venezuela and across the Brazilian Amazon into Peru. The plan was to return home from there in August.

On 30 May they picked up mail in Lima and in early June visited a place called Tingo Maria in Huanuco province, a site on the east side of the Andes in north-central Peru, known to be rich in birds of lower-altitude Andean forest. The story of what happened next was largely pieced together with the help of a Peruvian journalist and the Anglican bishop of Lima. While it passes more or less as fact, the precise details may never be known.

Apparently Tim and Mike set off to birdwatch close to the river almost immediately on arrival at Tingo Maria on 4 June. As they went a group of locals gesticulated to them in a state of some alarm. But since Mike and Tim were not Spanish speakers they misunderstood or ignored the nature of the warning. It was apparently a much more urgent echo of the advice, which had circulated amongst birders and travellers in general, that Tingo Maria was a no-go zone because of the activities of guerrilla fighters belonging to the Peruvian Marxist group, Sendero Luminoso, the Shining Path.

A group of armed Sendero activists appeared suddenly and attempted to lead them away at gunpoint. One of the two Britons, the taller, presumed to be Tim, tried to make a run for it and was gunned down as he fled. The body apparently fell in the river and floated away. The surviving Briton was then taken to the Shining Path camp, where they encouraged him to confess that he was either a CIA or US drug-enforcement agent. The bird guides and the notebooks and the English accent seemingly counted for little, because at some point the captive was liberally fed and watered, then shot. No bodies were ever recovered.

Comparisons between such kinds of tragedy are pointless. The events are meaningful only in terms of their impact upon ourselves. Yet one of the most difficult things about what befell Alan Adams, and then Tim and Mike, is not knowing. In some ways I feel that what happened in Nepal is even worse than that which occurred at Tingo Maria. At least in Peru there was the semblance of a story. In Nepal there was no trace, no rumour, no hearsay report, certainly no body – nothing – to indicate what happened to Alan after he walked out of that hut at Tharepati on the evening of 14 May 1983.

Yet the facts surrounding his disappearance are simple enough. Clive and Toby became increasingly alarmed as night fell and Alan failed to return. They left the hut and bellowed his name across the hillside. But there was no possibility of searching for him in the pitch dark and that night there was a massive lightning storm, which turned to snow and left a white skin of frost across the landscape by dawn.

They were in turmoil as they pondered the consequences of these conditions. Alan had been wearing only a jumper and T-shirt. His two companions doubted anyone could have survived the night without proper cold-weather equipment.

When the shadows closed in on the solitary flame-lit hut, Clive and Toby were also genuinely fearful that if Alan had fallen into evil hands, then they might be next.

All the following morning they continued to hunt for him and increasingly widened the field of the search. A group of ten passing New Zealanders pitched in for a couple of hours, but when they left Clive and Toby realised they needed extra manpower and dropped down several thousand feet to the nearest village to summon more help. Only two local people offered their services. The rest declined, either afraid of official repercussions once the story got out, or out of fearful superstition that the white man's death would result in bad karma for all concerned.

The four of them now continued to comb the steep hillsides and dense forest for a further two days, but all the time their thoughts were grinding inexorably to a single conclusion. The night he vanished he couldn't really have gone very far intentionally. He wasn't equipped and he didn't have time. In that case, he should have been within earshot of their shouts even on that first evening. The fact that he had not responded led to the inevitable presumption that he had never been able to hear them.

The slopes just beneath Tharepati are extremely steep, some so precipitous that Clive and Toby couldn't even descend to search, while the soles of Alan's Doc Martens had been worn as smooth as glass by six months' continual use. Setting aside the highly unlikely possibility of attack from leopard, bear or human, they thought it most likely that Alan had slipped to his death.

After more days of searching had turned up nothing, they made a two-day route march back to Kathmandu to report Alan's disappearance and instigate an official search. But it was a forlorn process. The British embassy shrugged it off, more concerned with who should pay for a manhunt than how they might mount one. The Nepalese police simply waved in Clive's face a thick sheaf of papers relating to the scores of tourists who had gone missing in the mountains. As far as his two friends knew no official lifted so much as a finger for Alan. Drained and weary, unable to do anything positive except notify family and friends back home, Clive and Toby felt they had reached the end of the road.

I only learnt of Alan's disappearance once I had arrived back in Britain at the end of May. It was pretty clear what the final dénouement had been and it had a terrible effect. Throughout the summer of 1983 I had a recurring nightmare. In the middle of the night, surfacing from a sickly half-sleep I'd sit bolt upright as if struck by an electric current, wringing wet and heart pounding, without really understanding what it was that had disturbed me. Perhaps I was dying over and over again with Alan as I tried to grapple with those last terrible imponderables: What could have happened? Why had it occurred? Why was there no trace of him? And, most irrationally – since I was in Varanasi on that dreadful night – could I have done anything about it?

For some time I harboured a fanciful kind of Shangri-La image of him wandering across the Himalayas alone, where he would be living safe and well in Tibet. Other slightly less improbable stories eventually bubbled to the surface – his clothes had been seen in the nearby town of Trisuli Bazaar; a single Doc Marten boot had been found near the Langtang–Gosainkund trail several years later – but none of these reports was traceable to one hard fact.

For thirteen years it remained one of the heart's unclosed doors. Partly to lay some of the ghosts to rest, partly to pay some kind of respects, I organised a trip to the Langtang area in May 1996. On the late afternoon that we reached Tharepati it seemed a forsaken place and while we were scheduled to pass the night, I found it too haunted to stay and we moved on another two hours' walk before stopping to camp in the evening mist and rain.

Yet one of the trip's objectives had been fulfilled. Just two days earlier at Chandan Bari, for three or four glorious seconds, a Satyr Tragopan had remained on its tree stump, the spot where it had greeted the dawn with that eerie drawn-out wail. *W-a-a-a-a-a-a-a.*

By 1996 the bird was many things to me. In fact, more than any other bird. Even in 1982–3 it had been the leitmotif of our trip. Alan had described it in a letter to a friend as 'the glittering prize'. Since his disappearance it had become overburdened with emotional significance. It was, after all, the creature he'd been searching for on the night he vanished. So seeing a Satyr Tragopan felt in some ways like an act of restitution, not just for me but for both of us. The door was now closed. As Alan himself would have said, that wonderful bird was the end.

19

Back on Full Bonus

25 displaying Great Bustards, Otis tarda
Valdesalor, Extremadura, Spain, 14 April 1993

In times of great stress birders usually make one of two responses. Either they temporarily abandon birding – a condition known as having *fazed* – or they bird more intensively than ever. I've tried both therapies and definitely favour the latter.

That was exactly what Alan himself had done when he set off for India in December 1982. Just the previous year his mother had died of cancer and he and his father had fallen out. Alan had left the family home and had been living with his favourite aunt. To make matters worse, he had been viciously beaten up outside a nightclub and left unconscious in a back alley. Ironically, it was the compensation paid to him for this attack that had financed his trip to Asia.

Now I sense that we need the therapeutic effects of birding ourselves. But the place we're going is one I visited ten years after Alan's disappearance – the central plains of Spain, my favourite spot in all Europe and one which has given me some of my most memorable birding experiences.

There were eight of us, including several of the group who would go with me three years later to Nepal to look for Satyr Tragopan and visit the spot where Alan disappeared. During the Spanish trip we had spent three days at the Parque Nacional de

Coto de Doñana, then we drove north for the Extremaduran city of Cáceres.

It was a miserable day. The clouds had gathered all morning and by the time we reached Seville it was raining. Before you can ascend on to the tableland of the Spanish interior the road meanders slowly upwards through the Sierra Morena, passing through a sequence of sleepy picturesque hill towns – El Ronquillo, Santa Olalla de Cala, Monesterio, Fuente de Cantos – each a labyrinth of narrow streets reduced by speed to a two-tone abstract of white stucco and terracotta roof tiles. It was a miserable day, but it was an atmospheric drive.

The road north, the N630, was peppered with slow-moving lorry traffic and our two cars were soon parted as we took our rare chances to overtake. But we had a rendezvous point and we ploughed on, settling in to the relaxed mood of the journey – a mixture of the close, humid fug of the car's interior and John Coltrane's easy, melancholic sax on a tape of jazz ballads. Yet outside it was wild and blustery. The sombre landscape of early spring cowered beneath vast tectonic plates of cloud that collided to create whole regions of gloom, or ripped apart momentarily to give us moments of a brighter and lighter atmosphere. And all this climatic drama regulated by the metronomic sweep of the wiper blades.

In defiance of the song from *My Fair Lady*, the weather actually cleared as we approached our destination. North of Merida the cloud lifted and the rain stopped. The landscape opened out as a hard bony steppeland, which stretched before us in a great ocean of grass. Extremadura is part of a huge wedge-shaped plateau that runs diagonally across Iberia, with its north-easternmost point around Zaragoza then as far south-west almost as Cape St Vincent in southern Portugal. The whole region should be renamed 'Bustard Country', because this great lozenge of Europe holds the highest concentrations of the birds of anywhere in the entire Palearctic. About half the world's Great Bustards and possibly as many as three-quarters of all the Little Bustards are in this area. These were what we had come to see.

But as we approached the site I'd chosen to search, I felt like a maths teacher a few pages ahead of the classroom brightest. I was under pressure. I had to spot the Rio Salor, close to the hamlet of Valdesalor, then navigate us west from this location via a maze of farm tracks that all seemed to head out onto the steppe area marked in my notes as the place to see bustards. I'd never been there before, the Rio Salor turned out to be a trickle, while the bridge across it was no more than a rain culvert. We didn't so much drive through Valdesalor as run over it. Yet these things were quickly corrected, and there remained only the confusion over which track to take.

We followed each in turn until it was clear it was taking us in the wrong direction. Then we returned to the one that had seemed most unpromising. We kept threatening to ground on its deep ruts and it carried us straight into the yard of a large farmhouse. As we approached the laager of buildings, three immense white guard dogs the size of wolves came bounding towards us. They ran parallel with the vehicle, snarling and howling and I could see the black flecks on the underside of their pink lips and a set of canines that wouldn't have been unflattering on a grizzly bear. You might have thought there was little to fear from a pack of dogs chasing a moving car. Then I noticed that they weren't only keeping pace with the offside door, they were actually lunging at it with their teeth, grabbing and twisting the handle as they ran. I got the impression that these were carnivores used to getting their food from a tin can, one the size of a moving Citroen ZX.

Mercifully they gave up at last and left us to concentrate on our mission and the landscape. We rode up to a natural promontory that commanded spectacular views over the entire area and we knew we'd arrived. I think this part of Spain is a uniquely beautiful piece of country. The only place I've seen that looks and feels similar is the grasslands of southern Arizona. Like that American region, the Spanish landscape has a continental scale, only Extramadura feels bigger.

It was now late afternoon. The cloud cover had risen and

thinned to a fine blue-grey marbling across the heavens and the gently tilting bowl of earth on which we stood rose at the horizon to meet it, in a lip of dark pine-clad hills. Yet the plain surrounding us was sunlit and golden in colour. The rain had purified the air of the faintest hint of atmospheric dust while simultaneously dousing any possible heat haze. The total effect was a landscape of infinite clarity, in which everything from micro- to macro-scale was chiselled out to create a newer and deeper reality. Shafts of sunshine came down in strong diagonals as if the effects of gravity on light were momentarily visible.

It was in these perfect conditions that we started to spot the birds we had come to find. In the far distance were several vultures spiralling in the ether. Griffons are common and widespread in Spain, but a speciality of Extremadura is the much rarer Cinereous Vulture, the biggest, heaviest bird of prey this side of the Himalayas. A large female can weigh over twelve kilos and has a wingspan approaching three metres. It was one of these that we spotted cruising down on bowed wings to land in a few clumsy hops. And there it sat, huge, hunched, completely motionless.

Later in the trip we would occasionally see one close enough to detect the scrawny head and neck set within a collar of shaggy feathers, which stand up like a courtier's ruff. The head itself is pale and bare except for areas of black feathering around each eye. Superficially this appears as two dark hollows scooped out of a naked skull. The whole effect is a form of ghoulish majesty.

The immediate slopes as we looked south folded into a series of rock-strewn gullies and on the open shoulders in between these we spotted one, then two, three, four, five Great Bustards. With each scan we added to this growing tally until we could see a total of about twenty-five in the middle distance. The species is legendary as the largest flighted landbird in the world, an accolade it shares with an African counterpart, the Kori Bustard, which may just shave the record courtesy of a handful of really huge individuals. But big male Greats can be eighteen kilos and, given their reputation for good eating, it's perhaps inevitable that the species has been relentlessly pursued by hunters. This is partly why we lost it as a breeding species in Britain in the early nineteenth century, although it is principally habitat loss – the inexorable conversion of Europe's grassland into arable – that has pushed the bird towards extinction. Now it has the dubious glamour of extreme rarity to add to its intrinsic power and beauty.

But Bustards cap these attractions with a touch of bizarre theatre. In the breeding season the males indulge in the most extraordinary display. By a sequence of bodily contortions – the bird stoops forward to bring its tail over its head, the wings are virtually turned upside down and an air sac in the throat is inflated like a huge balloon – and by puffing out and spreading a pattern of white feathers, it converts itself from a chestnut-and-black bird into a huge sphere of white. The stock phrase for this performance is 'the foam bath display', which contains an appropriate hint of bedroom farce. Because the bird produces simultaneously, though I've never heard it except on tape, a vocalisation that can only be likened to a long, loud wet fart. Mercifully at 800 yards' range we were spared the note of bathos.

Instead our soundtrack was a medley of lark song from both Crested and Calandra Larks and it was the latter that dominated. It is reminiscent of the Skylark's rattling jangle of sweet and harsh notes but the Calandra is a bigger, beefier bird, while its song is correspondingly coarser. A friend has found the perfect image to convey the faster and more intense delivery when he suggests it sounds like lark song that's been squirted out of a bottle.

The larks were everywhere. No individual bird could be disentangled. The song of one knitted into the rolling pattern of its neighbour to form a seamless web of music – one glorious anthem that rose upwards in great vaults to roof the heaven with an indeterminate architecture of sound. You could easily feel that this song was without limitation, carrying on to the very edges of the earth. If this smacks of hyperbole, then we could accurately infer that the larks' unanimous narrative of territory, regeneration and sexual potency was at least continuous to the edge of the grassland habitat, to the very horizon of this glorious landscape.

Alan Wood, the same Alan who plotted my murder the day we saw the Satyr Tragopan in Nepal in 1996, was clearly as touched by these experiences as I was. He turned to me, as he usually does at moments of this kind, and said, 'Well, Mr Cocker, you're definitely back on full bonus.' He says it routinely, about once a day on most trips. It's Alan's way of saying that he knows I know, that he knows, in birding terms, we've just witnessed something special.

I was back on full bonus now because of those extraordinary displaying bustards puffed out as huge balls of feathers. White globes turning in measured, almost stately revolutions so that they resembled tiny planets circling in their own ancient orbit – a galaxy of larksong and rain-sweetened grass. We were saturated by the harmony and beauty of that place. It was a moment I knew at the time, neither I nor they would ever forget. It was special. It was wonderful. It was, dare I say it, holy. It felt as if we were in the presence of something larger. A god. A bird god.

Looking around and taking it all in, I remember thinking to myself. Birding. This is what it's *all* about.

Useful Information, Addresses and Organisations

BirdLife International

The oldest international bird conservation organisation in the world, made up of a federation of national partners. The RSPB (see below) is the UK partner. Through this global alliance BirdLife initiates major research projects and produces a wide range of authoritative publications on the conservation of birds and their habitats. It monitors the fortunes of the world's rarest birds in an important series of Red Data Books. Its headquarters is at Wellbrook Court, Girton Road, Cambridge CB3 oNA. Tel: 01223 277318.

British Ornithologists' Union

The BOU, the old spiritual home of British birders, organises a range of major conferences, and funds conservation research both in Britain and internationally. It is frequently consulted by the statutory agencies. The BOU Rarities Committee is the official keeper of the British list. *The Ibis*, now 142 years old, is one of the most important journals in scientific ornithology. BOU, c/o Natural History Museum, Akeman Street, Tring, Herts HP23 6AP. Tel: 01442 890080. http://www.bou.org.

British Trust for Ornithology

The BTO is the lead research agency on British birds and is a unique partnership between its professional staff and about 30,000 amateur volunteers. Maintains long-term studies of breeding bird populations. Various categories of membership give access to the bi-monthly *BTO News* and the thrice yearly journal *Bird Study*. The Garden Birdwatch scheme gives the most inexperienced beginner an opportunity to take part in meaningful population studies. BTO, The Nunnery, Thetford, Norfolk IP24 2PU. Tel: 01842 750050. Website http://www.bto.org.

Regional Bird Societies

There are four UK-based bird clubs specialising in different regions of the world. All are similar in character with biennial journals/bulletins and conservation funds that support research and other environmental projects in their targeted region.

African Bird Club, c/o BirdLife International (address above).

Neotropical Bird Club, c/o The RSPB (address below).

Oriental Bird Club, c/o The RSPB (address below).

Ornithological Society of the Middle East, c/o The RSPB (address below).

Royal Society for the Protection of Birds

With over one million members the RSPB is the largest wildlife NGO in Europe. It has about 150 reserves and has been working for the conservation of birds and their habitats for over 112 years. *Every* British birder should be a member. The Lodge, Sandy, Bedfordshire SG19 2DL. Tel: 01767 680551. Website http://www.rspb.org.uk.

British Birds

This monthly journal has run since the early years of the twentieth century and its 92 volumes are a perfect measure of the cultural and social changes that have occurred in the birding world since that time. Still essential reading. The Banks, Mountfield, Nr Robertsbridge, East Sussex TN32 5JY. Tel: 01580 882039. Website http://www.britishbirds.co.uk.

Birding World

First appeared as *Twitching* in 1987 and then changed to its current title. It's the other major monthly journal and has helped shape the modern birding scene. Mainly for those interested in identification and rare birds in Britain. Stonerunner, Coast Road, Cley next the Sea, Holt, Norfolk NR25 7RZ. Tel: 01263 741139. Website http://www.birdingworld.co.uk.

Information

There are two up-to-the-minute sources of information on birds present in Britain. Two companies rent pagers carrying the latest sightings of rare and unusual birds across the country.

Birdnet, 5 London Road, Buxton, Derbyshire SK17 9PA. Tel: 01298 73052. Website http://www.birdnet.ltd.uk.

Rare Bird Alert, 17 Keswick Close, Norwich NR4 6UW. Tel: 01603 456789. Website http://www.rarebirdalert.co.uk.

Birdline

The other option is to ring one of the eight Birdline premium-rate numbers. The first of these covers the most exciting rarities from across the whole country. The following seven cover rarities and any other birds of note in their specific region.

Birdline   09068 700222

Scotland	09068 700234
South-East England	09068 700240
South-West England	09068 700241
East Anglia	09068 700245
North-East England	09068 700246
Midlands	09068 700247
Wales	09068 700248
North-West England	09068 700249

The Birdwatcher's Yearbook and Diary edited by John Pemberton (Buckingham Press) is an invaluable almanac on all aspects of British and international birding. Carries details on every single bird society, club and initiative in the country.

Further Reading

Here's my top ten currently available bird books. All are published in London unless otherwise stated.

Beebe, W., *A Monograph of the Pheasants*, Dover, New York, 1990.
A recent two-part reprint of the original 1926 four-volume work. Written in a narrative style long since vanished from modern bird literature and with 90 plates of some of the world's most beautiful birds. A truly magnificent book.

Cambell, B. and Lack, E., *A Dictionary of Birds*, T. and A.D. Poyser, 1985.
A wonderful, authoritative encyclopaedia on all aspects of ornithology.

Cramp, S. (ed.), *Handbook of the Birds of Europe, the Middle East and North Africa*, Oxford University Press, Oxford, 1977–94.
I have a love/hate relationship with this outstanding nine-volume series. Known more popularly as *BWP* (Birds of the

Western Palearctic), it's the most complete text on the birds of our region, but in places it's horribly indigestible.

del Hoyo, J., Elliott, A. and Sargatal, J. (eds), *Handbook of the Birds of the World*, Lynx, Barcelona, 1992–2001.
Brilliantly conceived, sumptuously illustrated and very expensive – ten volumes will cost about £1000 – but still a book to set any birder dreaming.

Ennion, E., *The Living Birds of Eric Ennion*, Gollancz, 1982.
No longer in print and therefore technically outside the criteria for this list, but who could omit this perfect introduction to the work of the twentieth century's master bird artist?

Fry, H., Keith, S. and Urban, E. (eds), *The Birds of Africa*, Academic Press, 1982–2000.
A wonderful book and although much less detailed than *BWP* a far more accessible regional work. When the last of the seven volumes is finished it'll cover all of Africa's birds.

Gibbons, D., Reid, J. and Chapman, R., *The New Atlas of Breeding Birds in Britain and Ireland: 1988–1991*, T. and A.D. Poyser, 1993.
The last serious assessment of British bird populations. A vast body of data has been neatly synthesised and beautifully presented.

Grimmett, R., Inskipp, C. and Inskipp, T., *Birds of the Indian Subcontinent*, Helm, 1998.
The best handbook on my favourite region with over 150 plates to set the imagination wandering.

Harrap, S. and Redman, N., *Where to Watch Birds in Britain*, Helm, 2001.
Still the best guide on where to see birds in this country. The latest revised edition is just being printed.

Mullarney, K., Svensson, L., Zetterström, D. and Grant, P., *Collins Bird Guide*, HarperCollins, 1999.
Concise text and beautiful plates, this is the best field guide to the birds of Britain and Europe, if not the best field guide to *any* region of the world.

Index

Index

Index